"The Street Machine Nationals was the epicenter of the hot rodding world in the '80s and early '90s. For many of us that came up during that time, it truly shaped our minds both with what a cool car is and in what a good time is! I continue to be close friends with several of the pro street gods today like Scott Sullivan, Gary Buckles, Troy Trepanier and—one of my best friends—Billy Wooten. Those guys helped shape an entirely new genre of cars that I believe yearns to return to the mainstream today. As far as the good time.....well that should make for an entire other book! I am glad Toby has told this story, because in most cases, time changes stories for the worst. In the case of the Street Machine Nationals, the tall tales are ALL true!"

### Christopher Sondles

Owner of Woody's Hot Rodz, Bright, Indiana. Winner of the 2012 Grand National Roadster Show "Foose Award of Design Excellence" and the 2012 Car Craft Magazine Pro Builder of the Year

"The Car Craft Street Machine Nationals in Du Quoin: The home of automotive debauchery that would reach legendary folklore status. But more importantly to me, it is where the best of the best would come to show off some of the most radical and awe-inspiring pro street cars in the world. Du Quoin would be the show where the editors would come to photograph and feature these cars that would spark the imagination of guys like me. But more importantly, it is where us 'average Joes' could go see these kings of pro street cruise by, hear the blowers whine, walk around them with our jaws on the ground, and come away with a lifelong lasting impression."

### Steve Strope

Owner of Pure Vision, Simi Valley, Califonia. Host of Entertainment Radio Network's *Car Craft Radio,* three-time Hot Rod Magazine Top Ten of the Year award winner, featured on TLC's *RIDES,* and humbled disciple of Scott Sullivan

*"The Street Machine Nationals underscores the real car culture in America. It's about real cars and real car guys, building cars the way they like them; not gaudy tribute cars or product-laden SEMA show cars that no one in their right mind would ever build."*

### John Baechtel
Editor, Landspeed Media Group and regular contributor to *Hot Rod* and *Car Craft* magazines

*"I first attended the Street Machine Nationals in 1979 and met guys like Scott Sullivan, Rocky Robertson, Matt Hay, and Rick Dobbertin. I was just a kid, but through these yearly reunions, I built a great network of relationships with real car guys. My career would not be what it is today without the Street Machine Nationals!"*

### Bob Thrash
Design Supervisor & Fabricator, Cal Automotive Creations. Two-time Ridler-winning designer & Lead Designer at Rad Rides by Troy for 18 years

*"If being a 'car guy' was the spark, the Street Machine Nationals was the accelerant. It was on the fairgrounds that a new generation of street machine builder was born, and from those golden years in the late-'80s and early-'90s, trends and styles were shaped and refined, and still resonate even today. It was a three-ring circus, certainly—but with the added danger of bumping into something cool at every turn."*

### Brian Stupski
Owner and founder Problem Child Kustoms Studio, Higley, Arizona

*"The Street Machine Nationals was a life-changing experience for me. As a teen when the Street Machines came to Du Quoin, I was amazed at the craftsmanship it took to make these beautiful cars. I am so glad to see the Street Machines come back to share with my kids and family, and I am sure it will be a life-changing experience for many young hot rodders out there!"*

### James Smith

Owner of James Smith Muscle Cars and originator of the "Bring the Street Machine Nationals back to Du Quoin, IL" Facebook page

*"I saw my first Street Machine Nationals by chance in 1981 and I was absolutely blown away. I was hooked. I was there every year at every show regardless of location—Indy, Sprindfield, East St. Louis, and Du Quoin—from then on. The Nationals was like a magnet—it was THE show. It was outrageous! The Illinois Street Racers Association is thrilled the show is back and we will be there in force!"*

### Joe Carter, a.k.a. "SuperProJoe"

President of the Illinois Street Racers Association. Originator of the "I miss the good 'ole STREET MACHINE NATIONALS" YellowBullet.com thread

*"I can honestly tell you that without the Nationals, I wouldn't be building cars today. When I heard they were coming back, I was thrilled! Pro street never died, it just got modified! The Nats is and will always be the best show EVER. Toby, what you are doing is freakin' incredible—to have a book with all of the icons in the industry is like the holy grail!"*

### Mike Cotten

Owner of Midwest Images and organizer of the 2013 Street Machine Nationals Charity Breakfast Cruise

SENSORY OVERLOAD: Cool Builders, Hot Cars, and Wild Times at the Street Machine Nationals

Published by Chaplain Publishing

3104 County Road 7520
Lubbock, Texas 79423
www.chaplainpublishing.com

Copyright © 2013 by Toby Brooks.

All rights reserved. This work is protected by copyright. No part of this book may be reproduced or transmitted in any form or by any means, including photocopies or scanned images, photographs, or via any other means without express written permission from the publisher. All photographs used by permission of their respective copyright holders.

**Library of Congress Control Number**: 2013942822

ISBN: 978-0-9883532-2-0

**Cover and text design: NiTROhype Creative**
www.nitrohype.com

Printed in the United States of America

COOL BUILDERS, HOT CARS, and WILD TIMES
at the STREET MACHINE NATIONALS

by TOBY **BROOKS**
forewords by BRAD **FANSHAW** & TIM **STRANGE**

# Dedication

To my beautiful bride Christi and wonderful kids Brynnan and Taye. Hopefully I have taught you iron-willed persistence and the value of finishing what you start. You've taught me how important it is to stop and enjoy life along the way. I love you all dearly.

# Table of Contents

**Foreword by Brad Fanshaw** ...................................................................... vii
**Foreword by Tim Strange** ........................................................................... xi
**Preface** ........................................................................................................ xiv
**Chapter 1: Prodigal** .................................................................................... 22
**Chapter 2: New Kid in Town** ..................................................................... 30
**Chapter 3: Unmistakable: Scott Sullivan** ................................................ 40
**Chapter 4: Over the Top: Rick Dobbertin** ............................................... 54
**Chapter 5: Lovin' Every Minute of It: 1980-1985** .................................... 70
**Chapter 6: The Hay Team: Matt & Debbie Hay** ...................................... 84
**Chapter 7: Rock On: Rocky Robertson** .................................................. 94
**Chapter 8: Paradise City: 1986-1989** ..................................................... 108
**Nats in Pics** ............................................................................................... 120
**Chapter 9: The Business: Rich Gebhardt** ............................................. 170
**Chapter 10: Indelible Mark: Mark Grimes** ............................................. 182
**Chapter 11: Nothin' But a Good Time: 1990-1993** ................................ 192
**Chapter 12: The Kid: Troy Trepanier** ..................................................... 204
**Chapter 13: The Canuck: Al Hinds** ........................................................ 216
**Chapter 14: Mr. Nationals: Bret Voelkel** ................................................ 226
**Chapter 15: Don't Go Away Mad (Just Go Away): 1994-1998** .............. 236
**Chapter 16: Don't Know What You Got (Till It's Gone)** ........................ 248
**Appendices** ............................................................................................... 258

# FOREWORD

## by Brad Fanshaw

*"It has got to have giant rear tires, wheelie bars, a gear drive, and a Dyers 6-71 Blower!"*

Every time that my friend Mark Grimes thought of a new car to build for the Street Machine Nationals, it started like the quote above. Insert the car style and the specifics, because having a car at The Car Craft Street Machine Nationals during the heyday of pro street meant that you had better have that or something even more extreme.

I was a Midwestern transplant, the kid from Southern California who was uprooted as a teen and moved with his family to Omaha, Nebraska. Arriving in February, it was cold, unfamiliar, and had nothing to offer this surfing, skateboarding BMXer. I was convinced of this when we moved to Omaha, but it was there that I found the girl who would become my wife, a group of life-long friends, and cars!

I became fast friends with many car guys in Omaha. I worked the counter at One Stop Performance, cruised Dodge Street, and raced Abbott Drive. One of my best friends would become a legend of The Street Machine Nationals and a king of the pro street movement, Mark Grimes.

When I met Mark he had just taken possession of a new black 1979 Camaro. We immediately bolted on a Dyers 6-71, Centerline wheels, and a Herb Adams whale tail trunk lid. Less than two miles from his house the whining blower spit the head gaskets out. We went home and proceeded to yank the motor from his new Camaro. This was the beginning of the Mark Grimes reign and solidified my desire to build custom machines.

If custom cars were our religion, then "The Nats" was our Holy Land. In an age before the fax machine and the internet, we would anxiously await the issue of *Car Craft* that held the entry blank. When the issue arrived, we would fill out the form, write a check, and quickly hustle it to the post office. The question among my friends in the late spring was always, "Hey, did you get your entry back yet for the Nats?"

Our trips to Indianapolis and later Du Quoin began in 1980. There were more pro street cars than any of us had ever seen at one show. I'd been to the World of Wheels and entered cars many times, but at the Nats the cars moved, made noise, you could smell the fuel and often the rubber. The Car Craft Street Machine Nationals was different; it was a visceral experience.

The Street Machine Nationals made me realize that there was more to cars than cruising Dodge Street: cars created a brotherhood. Throughout the years, as I attended with Mark and my other friends, we learned the spirit of competition, how to help our buddies, and how to deal with humiliation. There is always a bigger dog and no matter what you build, someone will be coming to up the ante.

At the time, I did not realize that my path would lead back to California and I would become business partners with another King, the King of Hot Rods, Boyd Coddington. Together, Boyd and I would win virtually every award, some multiple times, create iconic cars, and employ others, such as Chip Foose and Jesse James, who would move the game forward. I would also find that the young kid, Troy Trepanier, whom I met at the Street Machine Nationals, would also find a career in building cars, winning awards, and wowing enthusiasts. Harry Hibler, the man who is credited with creating the event would become one of my best friends and a man I greatly respect.

Now it comes full circle in an event many thought had become a page in history. Du Quoin, Illinois, the site many remember as the only location the Nats was ever held, is once again hosting the event.

The Street Machine Nationals is more than an event. It can create friendships that will last a lifetime, inspire your path in life, and let you become a part of automotive history.

I am certain the next king will be inspired. Long live The Street Machine Nationals!

*Brad Fanshaw is CEO of Bonneville WorldWide, Inc., a company devoted to automotive design, products, and marketing. Most visibly, the company produces bonspeed billet wheels and a line of handcrafted CNC machined Swiss watches. Fanshaw has won countless awards for his design work and was previously partners with Boyd Coddington at Boyds Wheels/Hot Rods by Boyd. In addition to his duties as CEO, he is also currently the co-host of* Car Warriors *on SPEED and can be heard weekly on the* Street Rod and Custom *radio show on ERN Live.*

www.bonnevilleWorldWide.com | www.bonspeed.com
www.bradfanshaw.com

# FOREWORD

**by Tim Strange**

I've attended the Street Machine Nats since I was 14. It was the event to look forward to each year. Even before I had my own car to enter, I traveled with buddies and we would sleep in our car in the parking lot. It didn't matter if we had enough money for a room, as long as we could attend each year. I remember the fresh pro street cars with crowds around them five deep and sometimes waiting almost half an hour for a decent picture.

I drove my first car to the Nats when I was 17. Two years later I redid it (a '64 Chevelle) and won my first national award with it (runner up best GM). A couple of years later I had another fresh build: a custom chopped pro street '54 Chevy. It was at that Street Machine Nats where I had my first photo shoot for a feature in a magazine. It was mind blowing, being a 21-year-old and getting four photo shoots in one weekend.

All the magazines were represented—not only from America, but from all over the world. Some of our shoots at the Nats ended up in magazines in countries like Japan, Germany, Norway, and Australia.

The Nats were also about hanging with your buddies and girlfriends. The fairgrounds in Du Quoin that weekend always felt like its own country, a place where nothing else mattered except taking in all you could over those few days. I met friends at the Nats over 20 years ago that I am still friends with today.

The Nats were where you got to see all the hottest new cars, colors, wheels, and anything else hot rod related. The vendor row back then seemed to go on forever. The lines into the fairgrounds were crazy to say the least. Du Quoin was in the middle of nowhere, so there were not many hotels close by. We always had to travel 30-40 minutes away just to get a hotel—and even that far away, those towns at night were packed with cruising and cars.

When we were younger we loved to hang out in Du Quoin at night. As we grew up and got nicer cars, we were a little nervous of all the crazy nightlife and would get out of town at the end of day.

My buddies and I saw many crazy things through the years. Awesome cars, lots of craziness, people passed out in ditches, tents and campers everywhere—and yes, even boobs. It seemed like when you were 18 and attending the Nats, there were boobs everywhere!

Many years we would arrive to the fairgrounds on Thursday, to try to beat the crowds to get registered. The trailer parking area at Du Quoin on Thursday was almost an event before the event. This is where we would wind down from the trip to the event. We had just spent days dealing with blown motors and transmissions in tow vehicles, getting lost (no GPS back then), and just funny randomness traveling with a bunch of gearheads on a hot rod vacation.

The trailer area was where we would see the new stuff first, usually as it rolled out of a trailer. This was the era of the fairgrounds cruiser and trailer queen. We would also check out some of the awesome tow rigs some of the guys had. This was the beginning of slammed tow vehicles and lowered duallies. People would just hang out on Thursday with the fresh builds unloaded and have a cookout. I remember we used to hang out for most of the day in the trailer area.

For several years Rocky Robertson held a cookout at his house before the event for people traveling to the Nats. We went a couple times. I was probably about 22 when Rocky took me to his office and showed me how the business-side of hot rod building could work: sponsors, promotions, and marketing reports. He was one of the first guys I knew doing this type of thing with his projects and promotions. He built killer cars with huge exposure and traveled to a ton of events. I am forever grateful to Rocky for seeing something in me and taking the time to show me this. I have been lucky enough since then to have been able to make a career out of building hot rods for 20 years. I have appeared in over 250 magazines around the world, been used for national ad campaigns, and have had my own hot rod TV show.

It's crazy to think that it all started by attending the Nats.

*Tim Strange is founder of Strange Motion Rod and Custom. In addition to owning and operating his shop, he appeared on Spike TV's* Search and Restore *for 32 episodes and now serves as an announcer for Goodguys Autocross events. His impressive list of awards includes the SEMA Goodguys Trendsetter Award, KKOA Triple Seven Award, and the First Annual Elden Titus Design Award. His work has earned awards at nearly every major show in the country, including where it all began: the Street Machine Nationals.*

www.strangemotion.com  |  www.spike.com

# Preface

*I was eleven years old and I had no idea.*

My dad, a lifelong gearhead, worked all the time as a heavy equipment mechanic at a coal mine just outside of Harrisburg, Illinois. He would sometimes work four or five weeks in a row without a day off to earn all the extra pay he could muster to better provide for our family. For that reason, when I heard he had purchased tickets to the 1986 Street Machine Nationals in nearby Du Quoin, Illinois, I was thrilled. After all, all that overtime had pulled him away from home. We could have been going pretty much anywhere and I would have been ecstatic. I was just happy to get to spend the day with my old man.

I was eleven years old and I had no idea.

On the day of the event, we departed the house around 8 or 9 a.m. to go see what all the fuss was about, see some cool cars, and enjoy a lemon shake-up or two. My mom had opted to stay home, but she had still lovingly packed up a small cooler with some iced sodas inside for the trip. A pretty easy 45-minute drive from our house on any other day, we set out for the Du Quoin State Fairgrounds. We thought it would be plenty of time.

Boy, were we wrong.

That first year, we got hung up trying to get through the tiny town of Galatia (their "Old Settlers' Days" festival always seemed to be the same weekend), then got stuck in Nats traffic again before we got to Christopher, still almost 14 miles away from the fairgrounds.

In eleven-year-old distance units, that line to get into the fairgrounds was backed up for at least a gazillion light years. Dad and I were going in his blue 1980-something Olds Cutlass with American Racing wheels, and I vividly remember looking at him when we both first spotted that endless stream of taillights.

"Man, I guess this is kind of a big deal," he said.

Now going on 27 years ago, I'd still say that was one of the biggest understatements I've ever heard.

## It was kind of a big deal.

Motivated by the flood of emotions I felt in 2010 when I happened across some old pictures of past Nats, I realized it was high time someone wrote a book about the greatest car show the world has ever known. I was procrastinating the completion of my previous book, *Season of Change*, when I accepted the fact that that someone would be me. I have been at it ever since.

Having grown up in Southern Illinois, my summers revolved around the Nats. If I had had Microsoft Outlook back then, the only days that would have been marked "unavailable" on my kid calendar would have been Christmas, Easter, and the Nationals. I wasn't alone.

As best I can recall, I attended every show in Du Quoin as a spectator from 1986-1993. In 1994, I had built a mild custom Chevy sport truck and decided it was time to experience the event as a participant. The Street Machine Nationals changed my life.

It was kind of a big deal.

That's why these past three years have been so glorious, yet at the same time so very difficult to explain to my friends. The cool part has been the excuse to talk to all my favorite childhood heroes, the builders who created the cars I remembered from the show. I managed to track down (in some cases lightly stalk), interview, and befriend most of them. As a part of the research, I also had a reason to buy and look at pretty much every car magazine from the era all over again.

The hard part was trying to explain the project to my friends. You see, my family and I now live in Lubbock, Texas. Hot rods aren't nearly as popular here as huge, jacked up diesel pickups. The Du Quoin State Fairgrounds are over 1,000 miles away. The show hasn't occurred since 1998. The odds of anyone in my social circles even knowing about the show are pretty slim.

"You're writing a book? Great!" would be the typical initial response. "About what? Did you say a *car show*? Oh." they'd reply with that I'm-trying-to-be-polite-but-deep-inside-I-think-you're-crazy head tilt and nod. But calling the Street Machine Nationals a car show is like calling the Grand Canyon a ditch or saying Eddie Van Halen is a modestly talented guitar player. It just doesn't do it justice. You just had to BE there.

**It was sensory overload.**

If you WERE there, then you know. The sight of gleaming paint, sparkling chrome, and carloads of sunburned bikini-clad girls. The sound of surging superchargers, loping camshafts, and blasting '80s hair metal screaming out of Kenwood 6 x 9's. The smell of spent race gas, spilled bleach, roasting tires, and overpriced bratwurst. It was raw and it was organic. It was overwhelming and it was awesome. It was an unrelenting, four-alarm assault on all your faculties.

It was Sensory Overload.

I was obsessed. As a result, I emulated the behaviors of the pro street heroes I'd be writing about with just a little twist. Instead of polishing a tube chassis for 1,500 hours like Rick Dobbertin, I tracked down, pieced together, and purchased a total of 828 historic car magazines. Instead of installing three superchargers like Mark Grimes, I read 99,360 pages of magazine features. Instead of hand cutting a salt flats-inspired graphic mask for two solid weeks like Rocky Robertson, I conducted over 50 hours of telephone interviews with 42 individuals. I built two websites and two Facebook pages. I wrote 16 chapters and close to 300 pages.

And finally, mercifully, thankfully, I finished.

In the meantime, some wonderfully exciting things happened. Most importantly, the Nationals came back to Du Quoin. Old cars that hadn't been seen in years were located again. Plans for a reunion were made. But the best part was that the folks who made it all possible the first time around started being recognized for the contributions they made and for how they changed the game.

In short, it has been an exhilarating, captivating, eye-opening, and at times absolutely overwhelming task. But I couldn't be more proud of the end result of those efforts that you are holding in your hands at this very instant. But even better, I am thrilled that the show is back and I get the opportunity to share a most cherished piece of my childhood with my own family as I participate and attend.

My hope and prayer is that the Nats will go off without a hitch so that they can stick around for good this time. So do me a favor, please. Behave.

That goes for you, too, Rocky. ☺

# Acknowledgments

This book would not have been possible without the efforts of a tremendous group of people who I now call friends. Your contributions are all appreciated more than you could know.

First and foremost, I give thanks to my Lord and Savior Jesus Christ. I've been blessed with a life far beyond anything I could ever hope for. Your sacrifice and gift of eternal life in light of what I really deserve defies description. "Thank you" falls far too short, but it is the best I have.

Next, my bride, my publisher, my publicist, my business manager, my best friend, and my kids' mom all deserve extra special recognition and thanks. Astonishingly, each of those folks is actually rolled up into one incredibly friendly and smokin' hot little package I am blessed to be able to call my wife. I love you, Chris.

Chaplain Publishing's ace editor Kristi Hart deserves a medal for her tireless efforts to turn chapters around to meet impossible deadlines. My deepest thanks for a job well (and incredibly quickly!) done.

I appreciate the contributions of Brad Fanshaw, Tim Strange, Christopher Sondles, Steve Strope, John Baechtel, Brian Stupski, James Smith, and Joe Carter for graciously providing their input about their experiences at the Nats. Thanks guys!

This book would not have been possible without the assistance of those who kindly gave their time in order to be interviewed. Builders included (in alphabetical order) Gary Buckles, Todd Clark, Rick Dobbertin, Wally Elder, Steve Gantz, Rich Gebhardt, Mark Grimes, Matt Hay, Al Hinds, Bob Maynard, Scott Sullivan, Troy Trepanier, and Bret Voelkel. Others included John Baechtel, Joe Carter, Susan Davis, Tim Farley, Harry Hibler, Fred Huff, Raina Lenzi, Marc Melvin, Jeff Smith, and J.P. Watters.

Extra special thanks to the entire Family Events crew. Bruce Hubley's insights were invaluable and he and Mike Moore, Ron Carlson, Matthew Louck, and Jessica Hubley are all true professionals. It has been my privilege to work with them.

To those who worked in and around Du Quoin to get the show back, you have my sincerest thanks. Roger Beasley, Terry Flanagan, Jim Holderfield, Danny Holmes, Mark Johns, Richard Layne, Kenny Lentz, Andy & Amanda Meadows, George Norovich, Joseph Roach, Paul Roach, and Troy Russell and others were all huge helps in the process.

Thanks also to the Du Quoin State Fairgrounds staff. John Rednour, Jr., Norm Hill, and Jeff Mason were each tremendously helpful in both assisting me gather facts and seeing the show return. Thank you guys!

I also am appreciative to those who assisted in the data collection and research for the book. Jordan and Brittany Boner were instrumental in gathering up the old newspaper articles and helping me piece together the timeline of events. Thanks for your help!

No book about the Nats is complete without photos. Ceasar Maragni and Butch Pate both deserve my deepest thanks for their contributions, as do others who provided images including (in alphabetical order) Jim Brooks, Rick Dobbertin, Al Hinds, Rocky Robertson, Scott Sullivan, Marc Telder, and Annette Zimbelman. Also, thanks to Dominique Harmon and Barry Nelson at Captivated Images in Lubbock for the awesome cover shot.

Which reminds me—thanks to my little thespian Taye Brooks for masterfully recreating my initial reaction to the Nats when I was a boy for the cover of this book. Love ya, buddy.

I also offer my appreciation to my beautiful and talented daughter Brynnan. You endured Daddy's moods when he was far too often strung out on Full Throttles after all-night writing benders. Now we can finally go play catch. Love ya, kid.

Thanks to Brian Stupski of Problem Child Kustoms Studios for lending the authentic SMNats paraphernalia that was used on the cover shot. Thanks, too, to Dave Drake from Yahwear in Lubbock for hookin' a brother up with the custom t-shirt Taye rocked on the cover.

Thanks to my mom Sharon for putting up with the years of grease stains, piles of car magazines, and I'll-be-there-in-a-second-because-I'm-right-in-the-middle-of-fixing-something extended waits before dinner. I love you, Momma.

Last but certainly not least I give thanks to my dad Jim. Depending on the day, I have you to thank or to blame for my love of street machines. Few memories from my childhood are sweeter than those we forged while roaming the Fairgrounds on our annual trek to Du Quoin. There's absolutely no way this book would exist if it weren't for you. I love you, Pop.

*TB*

# chapter 1 PRODIGAL

Ceasar Maragni photo

## chapter 7 | PRODIGAL

*'For this son of mine was dead and is alive again; he was lost and is found.'
So they began to celebrate.*

*-Luke 15:24*

### The Morning After

It's an all-too familiar but still tragic tale. The rising sun's warm rays chased away the darkness as it carried with it the party that everyone thought would last forever. The kid who had it all—guzzling up the wild life at a dizzying pace on someone else's dime—was now all alone, facedown and filthy among the crumpled debris that gave testimony to one last night of self-inflicted hard living. Somewhere along the way, he had lost sight of the fact that this really wasn't as fun as it used to be—or that the people around him had changed, seeming somehow harder, colder, and even less restrained over the years. And without even really realizing it until now, he had squandered away everything of value he had ever held dear.

It was gone, and probably forever.

On June 15, 1998, a similar tale was unfolding in the tiny town of Du Quoin, Illinois. Home to the Du Quoin State Fairgrounds (DSF) and the Illinois State Fair, Du Quoin had also served as ground zero for one of the greatest car shows the world had ever known—the Street Machine Nationals—for the past thirteen consecutive years.

If you're the type to believe in superstitions, number thirteen would indeed be the unlucky one, as it marked the last of the era. The show had sought asylum in Du Quoin after being shown the door by officials in Indianapolis, Springfield, and East St. Louis. "The Nats'" reputation as an unsurpassed gathering of some of the world's finest street machines was only eclipsed by its distinction as the location of one of the nation's wildest and raunchiest booze-fueled motor fests.

After the gates clanged shut on a soggy and rain-dampened 1998 installment, irreparable harm had already been inflicted. With well over 1,100 citations and arrests on the weekend several years in a row, Du Quoin had had enough.[1,2] One particular altercation had left a reveler so severely injured from a late-night beat down that he had been rumored dead.[3] He stabilized only after emergency transport two hours north to St. Louis for advanced medical care.[3] However, it wasn't like such startling acts hadn't happened before. This just happened to be the most recent batch of headlines declaring the steady erosion of a once storied custom car franchise.

Although long-term marketing agreements were already in place to support the show for the next two years, and media releases indicated that the Fairgrounds had already been booked for the '99 Nats, those arrangements would eventually be scrapped. In response to a steadily growing tide of vitriolic vocal public opposition by locals, city leaders in Du Quoin drew a line in the sand, refusing to budge over a few contested particulars in the proposed 1999 contract. In a thinly disguised move that belied the increasingly caustic local sentiment toward the event, the show that had once regularly attracted 5,000 of the planet's finest street machines and more than 100,000 spectators was turned away because the show's promoters, Special Events, had refused to foot the bill for waste disposal. When the city stood firm and insisted the Indianapolis-based company pay up, negotiations soured. Neither side flinched. Threats to take the show elsewhere turned into reality.

It was gone, and probably forever.

## chapter 7 | PRODIGAL

### *Reality Check*

However, just like that prodigal son, alone and sobered to a painful and stark new reality, time has a way of triggering some serious soul-searching. Most fundamentally, what once had been an annual rite for street machiners and random partiers alike had been whisked away over a disagreement about who was going to take out the trash. At the same time, the desperately needed tourism dollars, estimated anywhere from $3 million to as much as $16.5 million annually, went right out the door with it.[4] Make no mistake, though, the argument over who would foot the bill for basic clean up served merely as a symptom of the fatigue both sides felt as a result of an event that had consistently worn out its welcome everywhere it went.

Defiantly, the show stormed off and managed to carry on for five more excruciating years. By the bitter end, the 2004 27th annual Street Machine Nationals was an emaciated and sorry shell of her former splendor, with just 791 cars and 14,738 participants bothering to show up in last-ditch Lima, Ohio.[5] Meanwhile, DSF opted to fill its summer docket with a bunch of small-scale local and regional draws including a gathering for Airstream travel trailer enthusiasts and a three day long horse show—not exactly the kind of events to pull journalists from every corner of the globe as the Nats once had.

Formerly the crown jewel of the summer custom car outdoor show season, the Nationals withered and died, leaving little more than fading memories and nearly two decades of magazine coverage to show for its tumultuous but spectacular life. At first it seemed a welcome respite. The show morphed as Special Events, later rebranded as Family Events, Inc., modified the formula into similar spin-off events in other reaches of the country.

At the same time, Du Quoin seemed content with her calmer, gentler late June nights without the surging whine of roots blowers, squalling screeches of burning rubber, and unmistakable wails of youth unrestrained echoing through her streets. It was like a fresh divorce with both parties

seemingly thrilled at the thought of never having to wake up and look the other in the eye ever again.

But like any once-solid relationship, time has a way of healing old wounds despite a less than amicable parting of ways. Ironically, efforts to revive the show actually started via a medium not even imagined when the event was first conceived. A now epic thread on Yellowbullet.com, titled "I miss the good 'ole STREET MACHINE NATIONALS!" was started by user "superprojoe" in early December, 2009.[6] The five simple lines of the post lamented the loss of the show and one man's hope that someone would bring it back, now over a decade removed from the date of the last event.

Like the show itself, the Yellowbullet thread started simply enough, but what followed was nothing short of amazing. Within three days it was up to 183 posts. Within a week it was up to 475 posts. By September 2010 the thread had exploded to well over 1,800 posts. At last check, the thread is still going strong with nearly 3,600 posts over the course of more than three years, making it one of the most active threads ever in the history of the popular Yellowbullet.com website.[6]

Perhaps what was and is so addictive about the thread is that folks regularly contribute stories and pictures of their experiences at the show, making it an ever-changing source of information that, even if you don't know the author, oftentimes sparks a similar memory in the dusty recesses of your mind. It was a simpler time. And it was a blast.

It also clearly illustrated that the growing nucleus of reminiscing fans were now older and wiser. Undoubtedly, there's still plenty of evidence on the thread and elsewhere of that rowdy and raucous past. But what also emerged is that at its core, Du Quoin wasn't just a wild party that happened to have some nice cars nearby. It was an annual family reunion of sorts for a nationwide street machining brotherhood and sisterhood. And while there is no question that it was all about the cars, it was also about the friendships—a fraternity whose only pledge requirement was to spend countless hours (and thousands of dollars) hunkered over a handcrafted iron and glass expression of individuality and artistry.

For many participants and spectators alike, it was an indescribable assault on the senses that left them changed forever. And even if it couldn't be repeated in actuality, it could be relived in the virtual world of a vibrant internet message board.

Also about the time the Yellowbullet thread had begun, Southern Illinois car crafter James Smith launched a Facebook fan page entitled "Bring the Street Machine Nationals back to Duquoin IL."[7] Like so many, Smith had attended the event as an impressionable teen.[4] Ultimately, Smith claimed, it was the launch pad for his chosen career path as a restorer of classic cars.

Like the Yellowbullet thread, interest in Smith's page was remarkable. Although started on a whim, within a few short months the page had over 3,000 "likes."[7] Local media took notice and talk of approaching Family Events began to grow.[2]

### *Cruisin' Comeback*

Initially, discussions with Family Events were understandably met with some skepticism. After all, despite a swelling cyberspace fan base, this was the very same little town tucked away in a quiet and remote corner of Southern Illinois that had unceremoniously shown Family Events the door over a $3,000 trash bill some 13 years prior. Many of the residents who so vehemently demanded the Nats' ouster still squatted at their same addresses.

There were political hurdles to overcome, as well. John Rednour, who had served as the town's mayor during most of the Nationals' tenure, still held office. His son John, Jr., himself a teen during the heyday of the event, had grown up and had become manager of the fairgrounds.[8]

However, persistence started to pay off. By October 2011, Family Events Vice President of Marketing and Communications Matthew Louck indicated that the return of the show was looking increasingly likely; however, there simply wasn't time to schedule the event for 2012.[9] Family Events founder and CEO Bruce Hubley had organized and attended nearly every car show imaginable over a 20+ year period. After much deliberation

and a fair amount of coaxing, Hubley had finally been swayed into thinking the time was right to stage a comeback.

"There is no question that Du Quoin was the perfect place for a show like that," Hubley affirmed.[10] However, faced with a jam-packed 2012 show season along with an equally full DSF schedule, Family Events decided to table discussion for a later date and consider re-launching the event in 2013. This would provide ample time to pull together a quality show befitting the return of a once-legendary event.

On December 11, 2012, after years of emailed requests, countless encounters of in-person pleading, and more than one occasion of shameless begging from hungry fans desperate for a return of the prodigal car show, Family Events sealed the deal, inking a contract with the Du Quoin State Fairgrounds to host the show from June 28-30. The date of the event was significant, as it paid homage to the event's historic and rightful place, occupying the last weekend in June for more than 25 years. Although negotiating just a one-year deal with an option to renew, Hubley and his charges had agreed that the time was right to bring it back home.[10]

But just like the prodigal of old, the return of the show was not without detractors. Just as the show's most vocal proponents had seemingly chosen to overlook all the negatives of the event and focus on the cherished memories of iconic cars, good friends, and all around great times, haters chose to point out the public drunkenness, bared breasts, and senseless violence. Although decidedly smaller in number than the group who helped run the show out of town in '98, naysayers claimed that an older and wiser event was an impossibility. However, those relatively isolated complaints aside, overall, sentiment both locally and across multiple websites was overwhelmingly positive.

And why not? After all, the show was dead and now it was alive. It was lost and now it was found. And just like that first time in 1986, it was time to celebrate.

## References

1. Kern K. Ranbow's End at Nationals. *Du Quoin Evening Call*. June 15, 1998: 1-2.
2. Stewart B. Street Machine Nationals look more likely. *The Southern Illinoisan*. October 14, 2011.
3. Croessman J. Du Quoin Beating Victim in Fair Condition After Weekend Attack. *Du Quoin Evening Call*. June 16, 1998.
4. Stewart B. Street Machine Nationals might make a comeback. *The Southern Illinoisan*. August 18, 2011.
5. Family Events. 2004 Street Machine Nationals Results. http://web.archive.org/web/20051125073630/http://www.familyevents.com/results/results.asp?c=1&i=15. Accessed March 16, 2012.
6. Carter J. I miss the good 'ole STREET MACHINE NATIONALS! 2009; http://www.yellowbullet.com/forum/showthread.php?t=193327. Accessed June 29, 2011.
7. Smith J. Bring the Street Machine Nationals back to Duquoin IL. 2011; http://www.facebook.com/pages/Bring-the-Street-Machine-Nationals-back-to-Duquoin-IL/144469858961895?fref=ts. Accessed February 15, 2013.
8. Eisenhauer A. Street Machines. *The Southern Illinoisan*. December 11, 2012.
9. Stewart B. Return of Street Machines looks like a possibility. *The Southern Illinoisan*. October 28, 2011.
10. Hubley B. Founder and CEO of Family Events, Inc. Personal communication: Telephone interview. May 22, 2012.

# chapter 2
# NEW KID IN TOWN

## chapter 2 | NEW KID IN TOWN

*There's talk on the street; it sounds so familiar*
*Great expectations, everybody's watching you*
*People you meet, they all seem to know you*
*Even your old friends treat you like you're something new*

"New Kid in Town," by Don Henley, Glenn Frey and J.D. Souther; © copyright 1976, EMI Music Publishing, Warner Chappell Music, Inc.[1]

### The Birth of the Street Machine Nationals

In many ways, 1977 was a forgettable year, especially for those with a love for high performance automobiles. Detroit was strapped with tightening federal emissions and fuel economy standards and still scared silly by the ever-growing threat of gasoline shortages. Two of the Big Three responded with such forgettable offerings as a 180 horsepower Chevy Corvette[2] and an 88 horsepower 4-banger Ford Mustang.[3]

The nation's stagnated economy was no help, either, as demand for cheap and efficient transportation overshadowed America's long-held love affair with horsepower. Domestic automakers—never before legitimately threatened by foreign competition—were relatively slow to respond, thereby opening the floodgates to Japanese automakers whose lineups were brimming with lightweight, gas-sipping models perfect for the time.

In what many have come to refer to as the "Automotive Dark Ages," the late seventies are a time many self-professed "car guys and girls" would just as soon never revisit.[4]

In times of economic trouble, it is usually the demand for used cars that increases. Consumers, fearful of their cash-flows month-to-month, typically prefer to save money and avoid splurging for a new car that loses value the instant it is driven off the lot. At the same time, young hot rodders and street machiners interested in enhancing the looks and performance of their cars oftentimes forgo the high initial expense of a new car, too. Instead, a more affordable used car allows the buyer to save money up front and divert those savings to modifications as budget permits.[5]

Many experienced car buyers point to the fact that purchasing a car that is at least five- to ten-years-old is a way to minimize losses from depreciation that comes in owning a newer car while still avoiding the value increases that come when a car's age make it a classic. With that in mind, many a used 1967 Camaro, 1969 Challenger, or other classic muscle car could be had in the late seventies for as little as a few hundred dollars. Would-be street machiners were willing to pay the hefty fuel bills to keep the inefficient thirst of that big block or Hemi slaked in exchange for their neck-snapping performance.

At the same time, the country was in the midst of significant social change. The decade of the seventies will forever be remembered as the coming of age of the Baby Boomer generation. Often maligned or widely praised (depending upon the source), boomers (typically regarded as those born between 1946 and 1964) were certainly difference makers.[6]

One key distinction between boomers and every generation that preceded them was their independence and willingness to be expressive in all aspects of life. The generation that ushered in the era of free love, Woodstock, and rock & roll also furthered America's love affair with the automobile. So, while 1977 might have seemed like just another ho-hum year in so many respects, a number of economic and social factors were working together to make it the absolutely perfect time to impact history.

With a car show.

## *Great Expectations*

To the uninformed, it may seem like a steaming pile of hyperbole to say that history was made when some folks decided to host a gathering of street machines in Indiana. After all, pretty much everyone has been to a local car show, right? You spend all day in the scorching sun, you clean and polish on your ride all day, a "judge" comes by to give it a quick look, trophies are distributed to friends of said judge (regardless of the quality of the cars), and everyone goes home until next year when we do it all over again.

Sound familiar? If you are like most, the idea of a car show isn't exactly something that sages will pen memoirs about for posterity. However, in 1977 America, the idea was perfectly timed and nothing short of brilliant.

It is probably safe to say that those who birthed the idea had absolutely no idea just how successful it would be. *Car Craft* magazine publisher Steve Green and national ad director Harry Hibler were together one day brainstorming with Petersen Publication editors for ways to increase interest in the magazine, provide a cost-effective means to generate feature articles, and better understand street machining trends as they were occurring nationwide.

The idea of a car show came up, and as Hibler recalls, it seemed to be the perfect solution to address each need. According to many, it was primarily Hibler's idea that ultimately grew through input from many others.[5,7-9]

"Hand Grenade Harry"—widely revered for his exploits blowing up dragsters and racing jet cars—was a 2002 inductee into the Specialty Equipment Market Association (SEMA) and a 2013 inductee into the International Drag Racing Hall of Fame. However, he says that had it not been for a Southern California rainstorm in 1968, he might have never even entered the publishing industry, and along with it, the Nats might have never happened, either.

Hibler had graduated from high school as a brash and confident 16-year-old in 1951. With a passion for cars, he headed to the epicenter of hot rodding and drag racing when the ink was scarcely dry on his diploma

by punching a one-way ticket on a Trailways bus headed to Southern California. Looking for work, he immediately went into the construction industry, promptly becoming a general contractor within a few short years.[5]

Working days in construction, Hibler began drag racing and midget racing by night at the age of 17. A year or so later he began working at the San Fernando dragstrip as a tech inspector and ultimately became strip manager for several years. As Hibler puts it, "I paid the bills through the construction business, but my first real love was cars."[5]

A chance encounter with Petersen Publication Senior Vice President Dick Day would change Hibler's path forever. "I did some work for Dick and his wife Joan. After we had some big rains in the area in 1968, a hill had slid down on their house and I repaired it. They kept on my case that I should leave the construction business and work for Petersen. I knew all the manufacturers and was really involved in the industry through my racing interests, so after thinking about it, in 1969 I took them up on the offer and went to work as director of ad sales," he recalled.[5]

While the idea of a national street machine show seemed sound, it would have to be executed flawlessly in order for the event to be deemed a success. The first major decision was where to host it. The Petersen offices were located in Southern California, and while the vitality of the street machine scene in the Los Angeles area was tremendous, the staff felt a So Cal address would make the event cost prohibitive and inaccessible to much of the magazine's core readership in the Midwest.

Indianapolis, Indiana, was the next location mentioned due to its centralized location, experience with large-scale automotive events, and relatively consistent late June weather.[5] "Indianapolis was very central to readership of *Car Craft*," noted Hibler. Most readers could drive to Indy, and a 300-400 mile radius around the city captured more than 60% of all subscribers.[5,7]

Facilities would not be an issue, either. The expansive 250-acre Indiana State Fairgrounds would provide all the room needed for a huge production.[10] And at least early on, the city fathers thought the show would be an easy way of generating added revenue due to its large scale.[5,7]

The Nationals were the first such show with which Petersen had been involved. Additionally, as a *Car Craft* titled event, the decision was made early on to limit entry eligibility to cars 1949 and newer, a bit of a risk for a first-year show hungry for attendees.[11] At the time, most of the larger local and regional shows around the country included both street rods (up to 1948) and street machines (1949 and up).[5]

Green and Hibler discussed the idea at length and thought the numbers were there to support a late-model-only event and limit participants to true representatives of the street machine movement—another decision that proved to be dead-on accurate.

This was not going to be your father's dusty old Model T or street rod show. It would be newer, louder, and rowdier.

For the first installment in 1977, a modest 1,300 participants and 10,000 spectators showed up to check it out and see what all the hype in the pages of *Car Craft* was really all about.[12] In just one short weekend, roughly 60% of the feature coverage for the next 12 months of *Car Craft* had been gathered and photographed.[5,9] Although turnout had not been astronomical, the show's promoters were encouraged by the vitality and enthusiasm of the show's attendees and thrilled that so much editorial content could be generated in just one weekend.[5,12]

Well-known and widely respected automotive journalist John Baechtel got his start in the industry as the Tech Editor for *Car Craft* from 1976-1981.[9] Unlike Hibler who was involved in the logistics and planning of the show, Baechtel was charged with covering the event as a journalist for the magazine. "My job was to attend and photograph as many cars as possible during the weekend," he said. Sometimes that meant as many as three or four cars at a time.

While Baechtel and other photographers would work over one car, owners of others invited for coverage would be polishing, preening, and preparing their rides to go next. "Our main goal was to bulk up our file of car features that we could pull from throughout the year. I usually left wishing the show were longer because I always felt like there were magazine-quality cars that we just didn't have the time to shoot," he recounted.[9]

In addition to generating feature coverage, the first Nats also featured an impressive manufacturers' midway to help participants and spectators alike see all the latest and greatest offerings in the aftermarket industry.[12] The show provided an unprecedented venue in which manufacturers and the magazine's advertisers could see the real power and reach of the magazine. Many such companies staffed their areas heavily and conducted pen and paper marketing surveys on-site. In a pre-internet world, it was quite possibly the best way to put those most interested in bringing new products to market in touch with the guys and gals who would ultimately plunk down their hard-earned cash to buy them.[5]

And perhaps most importantly, the stage was set for an even bigger event the next year. "The show served so many purposes, it is hard to really say which one of those purposes was really most important." Hibler recalled. Thousands of new potential readers were introduced to the magazine, and increased readership meant an even more powerful marketing tool for potential advertisers.

"It was a real conglomerate of ideas that came together and everybody seemed to jump all over it," Hibler concluded.[5]

Word traveled fast, as magazine coverage in the October '77 *CC* touted just how remarkable the first rendition of the event was.[12] The show nearly doubled its car count for 1978, with over 2,500 cars and around 30,000 spectators.[13] By year three, registrations topped 4,800 and spectator attendance was more than 30,000.[14] In a pre-digital camera age, *CC* photographers shot through 193 rolls of film and brought home enough content for more than 100 features.[14]

At that point, Petersen executives and Indianapolis police alike were concerned that the show was rapidly outgrowing the city's capacity to host and contain it. The March 1980 *Car Craft* announced that registration for the fourth annual event would be a first-come, first served affair with a hard cap of 5,000 cars.[15] Within three months, that cap was full and no one, regardless of car cost or quality, would be allowed to register for the event on-site.[16]

With estimates of cars turned away numbering in the thousands, potential participants realized that waiting around meant you simply wouldn't get in. "We used to Fed Ex in our entry form to be sure we'd get a spot," recalled legendary builder Mark Grimes. "If you waited too long, you just wouldn't get in," he added.[17]

In 1981, *Car Craft* offices were flooded with 1,600+ registrations within three days of opening and the show was full within two months.[9] By 1983, all 5,000 spots were full in less than 72 hours. Entry blanks were received via parcel post, overnight delivery, Federal Express, and virtually any other means imaginable.[5] The experiment in summer fun had become a proven summer sensation and a nationwide phenomenon.

## References

1. Sing365.com. New Kid In Town. http://www.sing365.com/music/lyric.nsf/New-Kid-In-Town-lyrics-Eagles/1CC971C9E434989E482568600021A93F. Accessed March 7, 2013.
2. Wikipedia. Chevrolet Corvette (C3). 2012; http://en.wikipedia.org/wiki/Chevrolet_Corvette_(C3). Accessed December 12, 2012.
3. Mustangspecs.com. A detailed history of the Ford Mustang. Background of 1977 Mustangs 2012; http://www.mustangspecs.com/years/77.shtml. Accessed Dec 12, 2012.
4. Borroz T. '70's Cars We'd Just As Soon Forget. 2009; http://www.wired.com/autopia/2009/04/cars-from-the-7/. Accessed December 12, 2012.
5. Hibler H. Former publisher, Hot Rod Magazine. Personal communication: Telephone interview. May 25, 2011.
6. Wikipedia. Baby Boomer. 2012; http://en.wikipedia.org/wiki/Baby_boomer. Accessed December 11, 2012.
7. Hubley B. Founder and CEO of Family Events, Inc. Personal communication: Telephone interview. May 22, 2012.
8. Farley T. Executive Director, Springfield Convention & Business Center. Personal communication: Telephone interview. May 20, 2011.
9. Baechtel J. Former staffer, Car Craft and Hot Rod Magazines. Personal communication: Telephone interview. May 19, 2011.
10. Indiana State Fairgrounds. Indiana State Fairgrounds. 2012; http://www.in.gov/statefair/fairgrounds/. Accessed December 12, 2012.
11. Caldwell B. Car Craft '77 Street Machine Nationals: Put Your Street Machine Where Your Mouth Is. *Car Craft*. March 1977:72-73; 103.
12. Caldwell B. Street Machines March on Indianapolis! *Car Craft*. October 1977:46-53.

13. Vogelin R. '78 Street Machine Nationals. *Car Craft*. October 1978:26-34; 106.
14. Smith J, Asher J, Britt N. Supercar Summer. *Car Craft*. October 1979:26-33.
15. Asher J. The 1980 Car Craft Street Machine Nationals is Coming! *Car Craft*. March 1980:55.
16. Asher J. 1980 Street Machine Nationals West. *Car Craft*. June 1980:78.
17. Grimes M. Custom car builder. Personal communication: Telephone interview. May 27, 2011.

# chapter 3

# UNMISTAKABLE SCOTT SULLIVAN

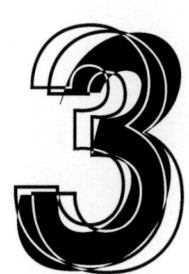

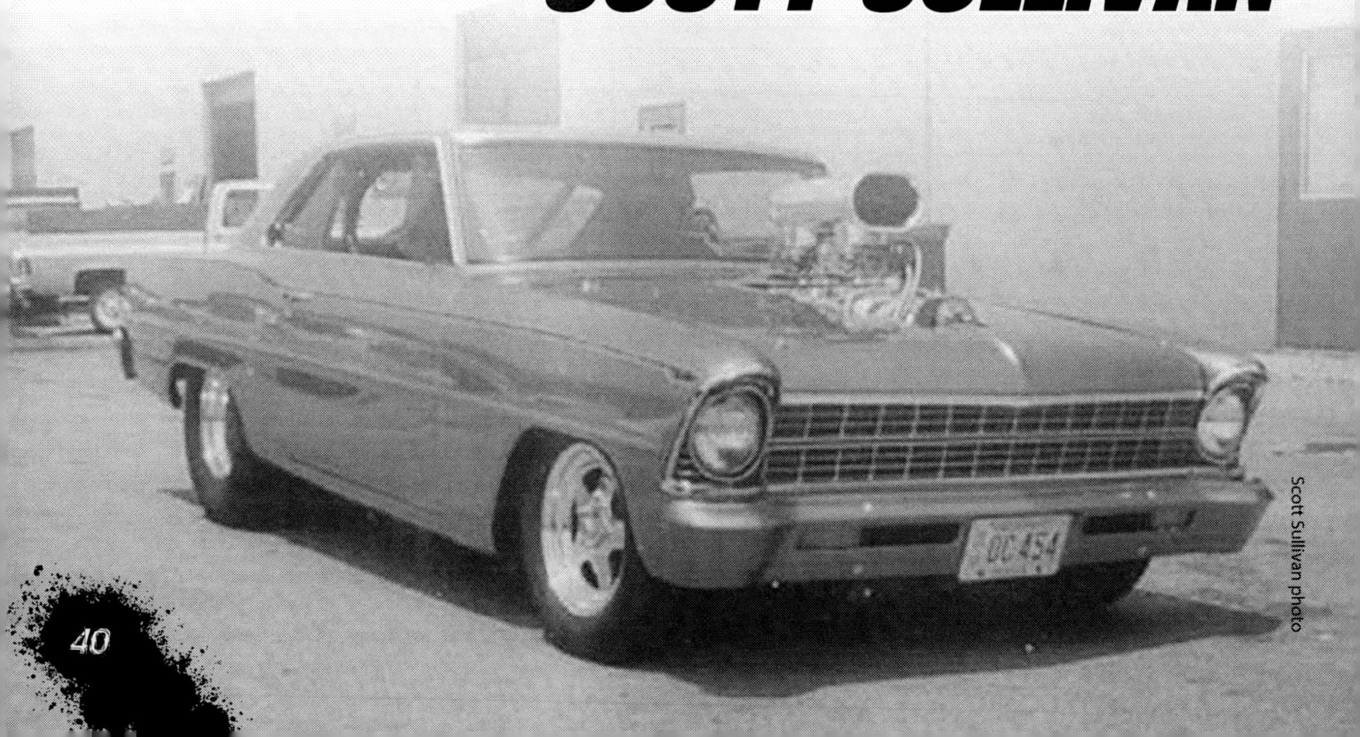

Scott Sullivan photo

chapter 3 | UNMISTAKABLE

*"I'm willing to go to any possible extreme to make it look like nothing ever happened."*

-Scott Sullivan

## Game Changers

**Y**ou might not have ever really considered it, but 1955 was arguably a watershed moment for hot rodding as a result of three things. First, Chevrolet dropped the very first Generation I small block engines into select 1955 model year cars.[1] The "mighty mouse" power plant was revolutionary due to its compact size and light weight. Extensive aftermarket support and relatively low cost to build, maintain, and modify the venerable design has made it the most successful engine ever in NASCAR, NHRA, and USAC while also being wildly popular in high performance street applications, too.[2]

In all, over 90,000,000 small block Chevys have been built with a fair percentage of those modified, tweaked, and massaged for improved performance. Speed parts and tuning tricks are plentiful, but it all started with 265 cubic inches back in 1955 Detroit.

Without question, the small block Chevy changed hot rodding forever. However, so too did the 1955 Chevy, one of the two cars in which you could get the new small block.[1] The first of three model years that have since become legendary hot rodding icons, the '55 marked a radical styling departure for the car first introduced in 1950.[3]

The "tri-five," also known as the "shoebox," was available in entry-level 150, midrange 210, top-of-the-line Bel Air, or Nomad station wagon models.[4] The car was an immediate hit with hot rodders, and its popularity continues to this day.

Although countless thousands of '55-'57 Chevys have been modified, customized, and otherwise 'rodded through the years, the American Graffiti '55 in the classic movie *Two Lane Blacktop* further cemented the car's place not only in the hearts of Chevrolet aficionados but in lovers of all things Americana, as well.

While the combination of the launch of the small block and the re-design of the shoebox Chevy both came out of Detroit, it was yet another debut some three and a half hours south in gritty Dayton, Ohio, that would eventually stand the world of street machining on its collective ear not once but *twice*.

And while the Generation I engine and classic tri-five design are both discussed largely in the historical context of what they did for the industry, it is the persistent contributions of this one iconic and legendary builder working out of a modest two car garage that makes Scott Sullivan unmistakable. It is also the reason why he and the cars he has constructed over the parts of five decades remain as pertinent today as they were when he first burst on the scene in the pages of *Car Craft* in 1974 as a brash 19-year-old with a 1971 Dodge Demon.

### *Out of the Pack*

Dayton has long been revered as a ground zero of sorts for the street machine scene. The subject of one of *Car Craft*'s "Cruisin' USA" series,[5] the city can trace its love for the automobile directly to its blue collar roots and relatively close proximity to the Motor City. The home to Wright-Patterson Air Force base and birthplace of the Wright brothers was also once home to a vibrant manufacturing economy in the first half of the century.

While much of that economy has downsized or otherwise changed, a quick check of the hands of a Daytonite is more likely to reveal callouses and scrapes than manicures and silky smooth skin. And to better understand Dayton is to better understand Scott Sullivan. While Sullivan's first feature car was that '71 Demon, it is without a doubt his iconic 1967 Nova that proved he would be a major player and trendsetter for years to come.

Sullivan still lives in his childhood home in a modest, well-kept neighborhood in the heart of the Gem City. He got his first taste of the street machine bug when he was a tender pup of only five years of age.

"In my neighborhood, across the street and a few doors down there was a family with two brothers, Jack and Mike Yahle. The oldest brother Jack bought a new 1960 Impala. I can remember standing at the end of the driveway just to watch him wash it," he recalled. "The only thing that ever interested me from childhood on was hot rods," he said.[6]

When Jack was drafted and shipped off to Vietnam, Jack's younger brother Mike grabbed the keys to the Impala and pseudo-adopted young Sullivan in the process. "I didn't have or need a lot of supervision as a kid and I loved cars. Both Jack and Mike were real motor heads and they just lived across the street, so I was over there constantly," Sullivan recounted. "While Jack was in the service, I hung out there *all the time*," he said.

Even better, Mike ran with a half-dozen or so friends who all owned and customized cars, too. Young Sullivan simply soaked it all up, eventually getting his first airbrush at the insistence of one of the friends.[6] If hot rodding was in his nature, the nurture provided by his neighbors served to further stoke the flames of street machine greatness into a roaring inferno.

A few years later, Jack had nearly completed his military obligations and word came home that he'd be buying a new car. While other kids in 1965 America were preoccupied with the Beatles, Cassius Clay, or the space race, the only concern on 10-year-old Sullivan's mind was which car Jack would be bringing back to the neighborhood.

"Mike told me that Jack had ordered a new 1965 180-horse Covair or a '65 street Hemi Dodge Coronet. I remember *praying* that the Hemi car came in, and I'll be damned if the Corvair didn't roll up to the house," he said with a laugh. "I was so mad I could hardly stand it. TEN years old, and that's all I could worry about," he said.

Sullivan attended the very first Street Machine Nationals in Indy in 1977 in a '69 Nova he had built as a driver for his girlfriend at the time. "I put four inch and ten inch Cragar SS wheels and built the wheel flares from scratch. I painted the car silver-blue and did some artwork on it. By the time I was done, I absolutely *loved* the way the car drove and I told her she couldn't have it," he noted with a chuckle.

Sullivan attended as a part of Dayton's infamous "Rat Pack," headed up by local hot rodder Pat Crafton. Crafton had built a '70 Chevelle for himself and a '68 Camaro for his wife. His affinity for big block Chevy "rat" engines in all his cars led someone to dub the crew a "Rat Pack" and the name stuck. "I got to know Pat and really liked him so we started hanging out," he said. The bunch got wind of the Nats and signed up right away.

For Sullivan, the first inklings of the pro street movement came as early as 1974, when he contemplated cutting up his Demon to put fat tires on the back to get that unmistakable pro stock look on the streets. Sullivan can recall lying on his cold driveway (he didn't even have a garage yet) with a big piece of plastic draped over the Dodge while a kerosene-fueled heater inflated a makeshift bubble to chase the harsh bite out of the nine-degree December Ohio air.

"I had it all jacked up with the rear end out of it trying to figure out how in the world to put 14 x 32 inch slicks on it." Although he didn't end up tubbing the Demon, it set the stage for cars to come.

## The Nova

Sullivan was in the market for his next project in 1977 when he came across an extremely well built 1967 Nova still sporting factory paint and a vinyl top. The car had already been back halved and set up for drag racing. In Sullivan's words, he decided he simply *had* to have it. Unfortunately, the car's owner had just bought it and had his heart set on regularly taking it to the strip.

"I fell in love with the car, but unfortunately he wouldn't sell," he said. "I told him drag racing is basically a bottomless pit that you just shovel money into every week, but he wouldn't budge," Sullivan added. Two weeks later the owner had a change of heart when he saw Sullivan's warnings coming true. He had grenaded the motor and decided he wanted Sullivan to come take the car off his hands. For the paltry sum of $1,800, the former "Buckeye Express" was sold as a roller and headed for legendary street hero status.

At the same time, Sullivan was also working to create a shop in which he could build the car. "I had convinced my father to let me build a 26 x 26 garage behind the house as long as I would pay for it," he stated. Sullivan built the modest shop and promptly went to work building the Nova for the '78 Nationals. And unlike the gazillion dollar turnkey builds so popular today, this was simply a man with a vision, a modest collection of hand tools, and a two car garage. Sullivan still builds from the same location today.

By the time the 1978 Nationals rolled around, the Rat Pack showed up in force. A tunnel rammed '70 big block Chevelle, a lime green tunnel rammed '69 big block Camaro, and a big block 1970 Nova all rolled out of Dayton headed for the spectacle in Indy.

So busy fixing everyone else's cars, Sullivan was forced to leave his own unfinished Chevy II alone and sulking in the garage in Dayton. "At the time, the Nova was candy red with a formula 5000 hood scoop, but I was the only one out of the group whose car wasn't finished," he said.

Determined to make a splash in '79, Sullivan vowed to finish the car and did what so many do for the sake of their builds: he sacrificed his hard earned dollars to transform the Nova from simply a nice street car into the 1979 *Hot Rod Magazine* Street Machine of the Year. "I had a really really nice '72 Impala lowrider that was my daily driver that I sold for $2,000. Then I turned around and bought a Dyers supercharger for $1,950," he said. After braving the "Blizzard of 1978" in a miserable $300 Pinto beater that

had taken the place of his beloved but sacrificed Impala, Sullivan hauled the blower home and promptly went to work installing it on the Nova. "I remember thinking, 'I had a nice car, now I've got a piece of s*@! and a big pile of aluminum,'" he added. Such was the price of glory.

Contrary to popular belief, Sullivan did not have the first-ever tubbed car to be featured in the pages of *Car Craft, Hot Rod,* or *Popular Hot Rodding*. In case you were wondering, that distinction belongs to a number of cars, including Vince Hill's Vega Wagon (Feb. 1977 *Hot Rod*)[7], Steve Lisk's 1970 Dodge Challenger (Aug. 1977 *Car Craft* & Sept. 1977 *Hot Rod*)[8,9] and John Carpenter's Vega GT (Aug. 1977 *Car Craft*).[10]

Even though the Nova might not have been first, it was unquestionably the most memorable tubbed car in the minds of many. Its timeless and tasteful paint and graphics, perfect raked stance, and wicked blown big block made it a trend-setting car that has never gone out of style, even today. That is certainly no small feat for a car built over 35 years ago by a twenty-something guy in his own garage.

Interestingly, Sullivan laments that despite the way the car has been immortalized in many respects over time (#20 Top 100 Most Influential Hot Rods of All Time, *Hot Rod* Magazine, among countless other top all-time type awards),[11] it debuted at the '79 Nationals without much fanfare. However, all three major magazines took notice and the car was subsequently featured in the October 1979 issues of *Car Craft, Hot Rod,* and *Popular Hot Rodding*.[12-14] Whether he realized it at the time or not, Sullivan was on his way to legendary status as one of the most prolific builders of all time.

After the three-for-three showing in all the major magazines in 1979, the car had become an iconic torchbearer of sorts for a pro street movement that was steadily gaining momentum nationwide. By the time the 1980 Nationals rolled around, people flocked to see the car they had read about in all the major mags.

"When we pulled in the gates, people were literally running to the car and screaming. It was like a mob scene. It was absolutely unbelievable," Sullivan recounted.

Far from a one-trick pony with just a car of his own, Sullivan kept right on building game-changing cars for others and his legend continued to grow. A 1970 Chevelle built for an old girlfriend ended up on the November 1980 cover of *Hot Rod*.[15] In 1981, fellow Ohio native Steve Williams approached Sullivan to finish off his 1966 Chevelle that had been treated to a chassis back half at Jeg's Performance. Sullivan recalled their conversation vividly.

"I told him straight up: give me $2,000 and I will make you famous," he said. Sullivan worked tirelessly to build his trickest creation yet and was able to enjoy a degree of artistic freedom that allowed him to really stretch the boundaries of custom street machining.

The car debuted at the 1985 Street Machine Nationals in St. Louis with a set of brushed Weld wheels and blacked-out trim (both firsts) as well as a flawless turquoise paint job with ground-breaking high-tech mechanical graphics. The car placed third behind Matt & Debbie Hay's Oldsmobile and Joe Gallagher's '83 Camaro.

The real tragedy wasn't that the car didn't win, but rather that it would never be driven again after that weekend.

"The engine lost oil pressure shortly after the show," Sullivan said. "That car went into a garage and never saw the light of day again. The last time I saw it was around 1995 and it was rotting away. The lacquer had all checked, the interior had mold growing in it, the supercharger and wheels were solid white from corrosion, and it was just destroyed. From what I understand, it is still sitting there just dying a lonely death in that garage," he lamented.

Despite its heartbreaking demise, the car was groundbreaking in many respects, even appearing on subscription cards for *Car Craft* for years after it was initially featured.

## Pass the Cheez Whiz

While the '67 Nova is usually the car folks attribute *first* to Sullivan, it is his Cheez Whiz orange 1955 Chevy that most remember *best*. Originally acquired in 1980, the car sat in waiting for several years while Sullivan attended to other rides. As the pro street wars at the Nationals heated up year after year, Sullivan decided in 1987 that it was time to focus his attention on the shoebox.

One of the first rules of order for the build was that the car had to be a driver.

Bucking the pro street trend that, ironically, he helped ignite with the Nova, Sullivan intentionally built the '55 using a less-is-more approach.

The car had no blower, no wheelie bars, no tube chassis, and no crazy kajillion-color graphics. It was a flawlessly executed 496 cubic inch orange monochrome middle finger to those who thought it impossible to have a show-stopping magazine-quality car that you could actually drive on the street.

"I never saw the sense in having a trailered car at all these shows," he said. While other builders like Rick Dobbertin, Matt & Debbie Hay, and Mark Grimes were all debuting increasingly wild late-model cars with multi-stage supercharger and/or turbocharger setups (and in Dobbertin's case a differential so radically narrowed it left no room for rear suspension at all), Sullivan decided to take a different path to recognition.

"I consciously made a decision. I wanted to build an old car with a single four-barrel and no crazy graphics that I would drive to the event and spank everything on the premises," he said with a laugh. After thrashing for parts of two years, Sullivan accomplished his goal perfectly at the 1988 show in Du Quoin. This was no small feat considering both Hay's pink twin-blown Thunderbird and Grimes' red triple-blown Eurosport debuted at the show, as did Rocky Robertson's super trick Buick LeSabre.

"You can't take anything away from any of those cars, because those things were incredible," he said. "Rocky Robertson's Buick Somerset was the first real electronic fuel injected pro street car and it ushered us into the computer age. Matt Hay's T-Bird was just beautiful. And Rick Dobbertin's J-2000 was just an unbelievable piece of craftsmanship," he acknowledged.

"The fact that Rick could make that thing start and even run with two blowers, two turbochargers, and everything else just boggles my mind," he added.[6]

Incredibly, even though the '55 is probably Sullivan's signature build, it was only featured stateside in one magazine (although it was featured in a number of custom car magazines in Europe and Australia). And even though the car appeared in two features in back-to-back issues of *Hot Rod*, the stories focused more on Sullivan and editor Jeff Smith's exploits, trials, and tribulations on their 2,000+ mile journey from Dayton to Los Angeles (the idea upon which the Hot Rod Power Tour would later be based) rather than the car itself.

However, as *Hot Rod* staffer Rob Kinnan put it, "It was epic, and it inspired us all to stop polishing chrome and sitting on lawn chairs, and start driving our hot rods."[11]

Despite the lack of significant detail about the car's construction in the features, one item did stand out. Jeff Smith's now legendary picture of the color-matching Kraft Cheez Whiz poured down the deck lid appeared in the story's first installment.[16] Although the processed cheese product was not an exact color match to the car (Smith added red food coloring to the jar until the shade was just right), the name stuck. Thankfully, the cheese product did not, as it was quickly wiped away immediately after the photo was snapped.

After Cheez Whiz, Sullivan built or contributed to the builds of a number of other vehicles that garnered significant attention in their own rights, including his own black '57 Chevy, his red '51 Henry J, Tom Davis' Beretta, Al Hinds' Beretta, and Rick Cox's Cavalier.

Probably the craziest and most incredible display of his graphics and airbrush skills was Todd Clark's "Dem Bones" 1968 Camaro that featured a two-tone purple and teal paintjob separated by some of the finest detailed skeletal graphics imaginable. The car debuted in 1993, which also happened

to be the first Street Machine Nationals event Sullivan had ever missed since the inaugural show in 1977.

Close friend and former customer John Spreitzer (who had commissioned Sullivan to build his 1956 Chevy pickup that was eventually featured in the November 1990 issue of *Car Craft*) had fallen gravely ill. As a result, Sullivan decided to stay in town close to his dying friend. "That was the first Nationals I had missed from '77 to '92." Oddly, he never went back again.

In total, Sullivan's work has been featured 33 times in *Car Craft*, *Hot Rod*, and *Popular Hot Rodding*, significantly more than his contemporaries. When you include show coverage and mentions of his work throughout the pages in various locations over the years, the sheer magnitude of his street machine resume is simply too vast to even calculate. To say he essentially set the stage and defined the trends for more than two decades of street machiners is no overstatement.

### Nationals Reflections

When asked specifically about the Street Machine Nationals in Du Quoin, a show that he attended for seven of its thirteen years of existence, Sullivan recalled one fact without hesitation.

"It was hot and humid!" he expelled with a chuckle. "I can remember renting a house trailer near Du Quoin that I was in with Bob Thrash and some other close friends," he recalled. "All of us—complete idiots—just laughing and carrying on in the heat. We had no shade at all where we were on the fairgrounds and we were huddled under a frigging bush just to try and get out of the sun," he said.

"Without a doubt, though, it was one hell of a good time," he concluded.

More recently, Sullivan has turned his attention to other, broader pursuits. A true craftsman, Sullivan bristles at the thought of being pigeonholed as a pro street builder exclusively. He still owns the '55 and the Henry J and currently has an ultra-trick Harley bagger and a custom painted Hayabusa motorcycle. Perhaps most importantly for fans of his work, he also has an incredible "metallic cardboard and cream" LS-powered 1954 Chevy nearing completion in the garage that is poised to redefine hot rodding all over again, too. Although it is tubbed, he refuses to concede that it is truly "pro street."

And try as he might to shake free from his pro street paternity rights, there is no denying that there is still a place in his heart for the style. "While pro touring is all the current rage, pro street cars will always be popular and here's why: correctly done, NOTHING looks more evil or bada--," he said.[6]

Come time for the rebirth of the Street Machine Nationals, Sullivan will be there and fans of his work can rejoice. After all, he is the undisputed king of the homebuilt, handcrafted street machine. His work has a true old-world, artisan feel that simply cannot be duplicated. And while his style has been imitated, copied, and applied with varying degrees of skill and success by countless others over the decades, no one does Sullivan Style better than the man himself. As a result, it is safe to say that because of Sullivan's efforts, no hot rodder who really knows his or her history can ever look at a '67 Nova, a '55 Chevy, or a jar of Cheez Whiz without thinking fondly of the man from Dayton who took the Street Machine Nationals by storm.

Twice.

So far.

*References*

1. Wikipedia. Chevrolet small block engine. 2012; http://en.wikipedia.org/wiki/Chevrolet_small-block_engine. Accessed May 17, 2012.
2. McGuire B. Horsepower Nation: Chevrolet's Small-Block V8 Celebrates its 50th Birthday. *Autoweek*. June 20, 2005.
3. Wikipedia. Chevrolet Bel Air. 2012; http://en.wikipedia.org/wiki/Chevrolet_Bel_Air. Accessed December 10, 2012.
4. Magnante S. Buyer's Guide: 1955-1957 Classic Chevrolets. *Motor Trend*. December 2006.
5. Smith J. Cruisin' USA: Dayton, Ohio. *Car Craft*. January 1984:62-64.
6. Sullivan S. Custom car builder. Personal communication: Telephone interview. May 18, 2011.
7. Dianna J. Hill of Beans. *Hot Rod*. February 1977:89.
8. Voegelin R. Street Charade. *Car Craft*. August 1977:54-56.
9. Dianna J. Sudden Death II. *Hot Rod*. September 1977:41.
10. Voegelin R. Yellow Fever. *Car Craft*. August 1977:58, 101.
11. Freiburger D. Top 100 Hot Rods That Changed the World. *Hot Rod*. February 2009.
12. Asher J. Cold Blue Steel. *Car Craft*. October 1979:55-56.
13. Caldwell B. Street Machine of the Year. *Hot Rod*. October 1979:20-21.
14. Emanuelson L. Pro Street Super Sport. *Popular Hot Rodding*. October 1979:56-57.
15. Kelley L. Street Freaks. *Hot Rod*. November 1980:54-60.
16. Smith J. Pro Interstate Part I. *Hot Rod*. December 1988:54-59.

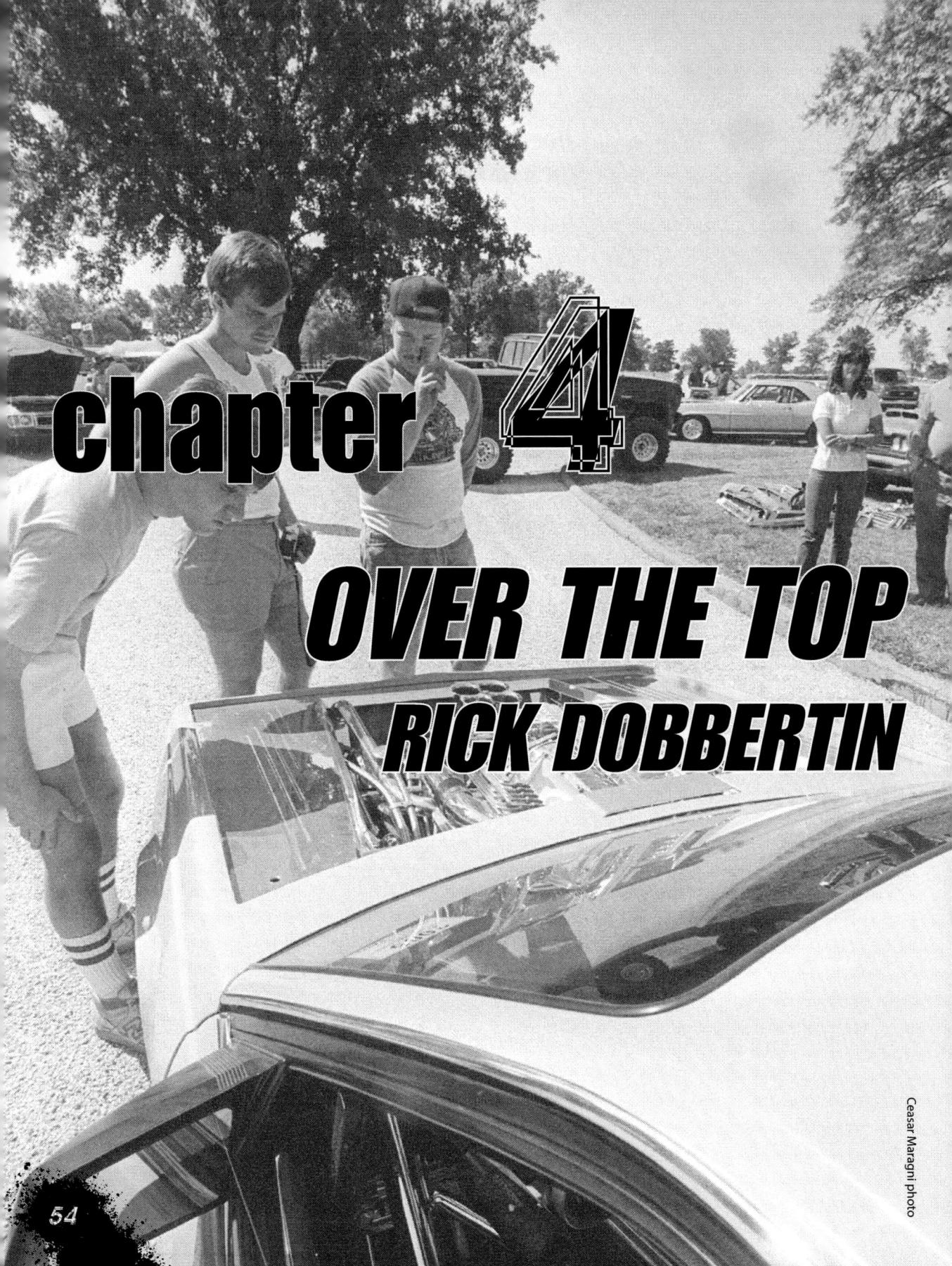

# chapter 4
## OVER THE TOP
### RICK DOBBERTIN

chapter 4 | OVER THE TOP

## *The Voice*

**F**or most people, actions are governed by an internal dialogue. We hear a little voice. During this conversation with ourselves, we decide whether to start or to stop, to stay or go, to try harder or quit. It is safe to say that Rick Dobbertin isn't like most people. And whether the voice in his head doesn't exist or he simply chooses to ignore it is inconsequential. The end result is that he pursues and achieves things most mortals wouldn't even consider and does it all with a fervor and passion that borders on maniacal. In the process, he has crafted some of the most incredible pieces of automotive artwork the world has ever seen.

Like all his contemporaries, Dobbertin started tinkering on anything with wheels at an early age. As chronicled in the March '87 *Car Craft*, ten-year-old Rick totally redesigned his Schwinn bicycle to convert it to front-wheel drive and rear steering.[1] Shortly thereafter, he turned his attention to four-wheeled pursuits.

"When I was about 12 growing up in Pittsburgh, I had a friend named Bob 'Oogie' Veiock, and he and his brother were always working on cars," he recalled. "They would let me and my friends from the neighborhood help out and get dirty, and it was fascinating to me," he added. Dobbertin says it wasn't the visual appeal but rather the tactile response that really set the hot rodding hook.

"It is an odd thing. If the first wrench I ever picked up, I would have said, 'Eww, this feels terrible in my hand,' and set it down, my whole life would have been different," he considered. "But I loved the feel of it, so it just went on from there," he said.

Went on from there, indeed. From bicycles to go carts and obscure import cars to classic muscle cars, Dobbertin's mechanical exploits grew and flourished as he did, ultimately leading to him being crowned the "Prince of Pro Street" by 1984.[2] However, by Rick's own admission, "good enough" was never good enough for him.

"I take everything to extremes, which in many ways isn't good," he lamented. And as trying as that character quality might be to an individual's life, putting stress on finances, relationships, and even physical well being, it is that insatiable drive for perfection that led to the creation of two of the most incredible cars ever conceived: Dobbertin's first feature car, a 1965 Chevy Nova with a blown and twin turbocharged big block, was the culmination of decades of refined skills practiced and perfected on other cars.

By the age of 23, Dobbertin had already built a number of vehicles for himself and others, earning a modest profit along the way.[1] He had settled in Springfield, Virginia, and opened Sandblast of Virginia. The company sandblasted everything from small automotive parts to water towers, then branched off to sandblasting redwood signs—but that soon grew too mundane.

Within a short while, Rick opened the doors of AA/Speed and Turbo Dynamics, specializing in one-off turbocharger installations and custom exhaust systems. During that time, Rick really began to refine his fabrication skills that would ultimately manifest with the debut of one mind-blowing creation after another.

"I had some T-shirts printed up for my speed shop that said 'For The Best BLOWN Jobs In Town....' on the front, and as tacky as they were, they also said 'Turbo Dynamics—Superchargers, Turbochargers, and Nitrous Oxide' on the back. That got me thinking about how cool it would be to put all that on one car," he said.

## chapter 4 | OVER THE TOP

As simple as the idea sounded, it wasn't without its difficulties, the first of which was finding a suitable starting point. He decided a glistening rolling billboard would be good for business. That's when plans for a radical Nova began to take shape.

Ever the perfectionist, Dobbertin looked at 18 different Novas across five different states before he settled on the pristine '65.[3] Taking four years to build using a no-expenses-spared mentality, the Nova was a smashing success upon its debut at the 1982 Street Machine Nationals in Springfield, Illinois. Dobbertin probably had to do some rearranging in the tub and fuel-cell filled confines of the trunk in order to haul off all the trophies he'd won for Best Engineered, Best Engine, Best Interior, Best Car, Best Pro Street Car, and Grand Champion at the show.[4]

What Sullivan's '67 Nova had done in 1979 in terms of raising the bar for pro streeters, Dobbertin's '65 did again in 1982 by wowing drop-jawed, googly-eyed onlookers with an impeccable attention to detail and the wildest induction system ever imagined up to that point. By the time the sixth annual SM Nats rolled around, superchargers had almost become commonplace. Turbochargers had been used, too. But Dobbertin's application of "all of the above" with pretty much every high-end high performance part or piece available simply dominated the competition. And just like Sullivan's Nova some three years earlier, Dobbertin's iteration of the Chevy II garnered full color features in all three major magazines almost immediately after the Nationals.[3-5]

The car not only changed the pro street game, it literally changed the rules. Prior to 1982, the Best Pro Street award sponsored by Competition Engineering had been limited to cars 1967 and newer. However, CE's Fred Gerle and other decision makers noticed Dobbertin's Nova at the event and thought it deserved to be entered in the competition. After a quick on-the-spot poll of other entrants to be sure there weren't too many ruffled feathers or bruised egos, the cutoff for entry was dropped down to 1965 and the heavy-breathing blue Deuce streaked away with the award.

The car was so revolutionary that upon its return to Springfield in 1983 for the seventh installment of the Nats, it again swept the podium

even though it was pretty much unchanged from its presentation the year prior. Such was no small feat for a show of 5,000 cars attended by more than 100,000 onlookers. The event had grown so popular that registration had filled to capacity in a little more than two days once opened in March. While *Return of the Jedi* was number one in the American box office, it was the return of the *Nova* in Springfield that stole the headlines.

### The Great Divide(r)

It has often been said in the music industry that artists have their whole lives to prepare for a debut album, but it is the sophomore effort that is the true test of an individual's or a group's real genius. The same could likely be said of hot rods. By the time the gates had closed on the '83 Nats, Dobbertin was already thinking about what he was going to build as a follow-up to the most heavily decorated street machine ever constructed. The first decision would again be to decide what car would serve as a starting point.

"The whole idea was to take everything to an extreme," Dobbertin recounted. "I wanted the narrowest car possible with the widest rear tire available. It was down to a Chevette, a Cavalier, a '49 Anglia, an Opel GT, and a Pontiac J-2000," he said. After settling on the Poncho, Dobbertin then literally wrote down every characteristic that was a part of what it meant to be a pro streeter and then actively searched out the most extreme possible iteration of that category.[6]

One of the biggest challenges was that a car of the caliber of the J-2000 would take years to construct. Dobbertin admits that he intentionally built the car beginning in 1984 with an eye toward what he anticipated would be popular two or three years later when the machine would ultimately debut. And make no mistake; pro street trends in 1986 had morphed. What started as a loose collection of ideas in the '70s about how to tastefully apply an aggressive drag racing look to a street application had somehow transformed into typical my-weenie-is-bigger-than-your-weenie alpha male posturing.

## chapter 4 | OVER THE TOP

What Sullivan had unknowingly done with his '67 Nova was change the game, and the message sent—whether intended or not—was that the only way to have a car so noteworthy that grown men came running and screaming like middle school girls who had spotted Justin Beiber in a shopping mall was to go all-out radical and build the wildest car possible. In typical '80s fashion, garish excess was the rule of the day and the crazier the idea, the better. The end result was more than ten straight years of a relentless stream of incredible cars built by maniacal craftsmen hell-bent on earning the crown jewel: Best Pro Street at the Street Machine Nationals.

The J-2000 was the result of more than 4,100 hours of skilled labor and construction at a total price of over $40,000 in parts alone. Adjusted for inflation, that represented a conservative estimate of $615,000 worth of labor and just over $82,000 in parts. At a modern-day equivalent of nearly three quarters of a million dollars aside, it was Rick's incredible—heck, most would say *maniacal*—attention to detail that set the J-2000 apart from any other machine before or since.

*Car Craft* staffer Bruce Hampson described it best in his feature "One Step Beyond," scooping both *Hot Rod* and *Popular Hot Rodding,* in which the car would later appear in *CC*'s August 1986 issue.[7] "Rick spent an average of 138 hours a month sequestered in a rented shop chasing his dream… divesting himself of virtually everything he owned of value to finance the undertaking," Hampson wrote.[7]

In addition to a polished aluminum small block Chevy with two turbochargers, two superchargers, a 20-port nitrous system, and a dry sump oiling system, the car featured a first-of-its kind totally polished stainless steel tube chassis. Each and every tubing union had been painstakingly welded and ground, welded and ground, and welded and ground again to the tune of 8-10 hours apiece until the metal flowed together like glistening liquid mercury.

The bare frame alone represented more than 1,500 hours of work. To put that quickly into perspective, if building the J-2000 chassis was your full-time vocation and you put in typical 40-hour weeks beginning on Janu-

ary 1, it would be mid-April before you did anything other than weld and polish 1 5/8" and 1 1/4" stainless tubes.[7]

The car also featured a Dana 60 differential so radically chopped that Dobbertin jokes he carried the 9 1/4" short axles around in a shoebox. By the time the mad scientist had lopped off the axle tubes to make way for the specially built 23 1/2" wide Firestone rear tires, pretty much all that was left was the pumpkin. In fact, space was at such a premium that Dobbertin says he actually trimmed the gear housing.[7]

Also revolutionary was the body itself. Featuring a flip-off front end and a pneumatically actuated body, the J-2000 looked more like an Autobot than an automobile when displayed for speechless onlookers. Dobbertin employed a wireless remote control to pop the shaved doors and perform other functions. Although such a trick is commonplace today, Dobbertin was one of the first to employ it. At one photo shoot, he says he had convinced *Car Craft* editor Jeff Smith that the doors were voice activated as he slyly pressed the button in his pocket.[8] After Smith unsuccessfully tried to gain access a few times, Dobbertin finally let him in on the joke.

Painter Chip Whittington spent over 1,000 hours prepping and spraying the car Chrome Yellow with 11-color Ditzler candy graphics.[9-11] The end result was mission accomplished: what *Hot Rod* staffer Rob Kinnan would later write was "the pro street car that would never be topped" as it took #41 (one place behind Sullivan's '55) on *HR*'s list of 100 Hot Rods that Changed the World published in 2009, some 23 years after it was built.[12]

When Dobbertin rolled the car off the trailer in Du Quoin in 1986, builders and spectators alike had trouble fully comprehending the gravity of what they were witnessing. People either loved the car or they hated it. It was an in-your-face sensory assault that absolutely demanded you pick a side between fairgrounds-cruising artwork or drivable street car. There was no middle ground.

As then-*Car Craft* editor Jeff Smith put it, whether it was built by Rick Dobbertin or someone else, it was the car that simply *had* to be done.[13] "It is human nature to take an idea and take it to its most radical extreme possible," he said. "Once you do that, you can then come back and either modify the rules about what constitutes 'pro street' or it leads to something else—and eventually I think it led to pro touring," he added.

For all that it was and for the fanatical manner in which Rick had built the J-2000 to surpass his Nova in every respect, it remarkably did not fare as well as the Deuce initially in show competition. Although Dobbertin won first place at the '86 Nationals in the Best Street Machine, Best Engineered, and Best Engine categories, he finished second in Best Interior and third in Best Paint. What stung the most was the car's second place finish in the highly coveted Competition Engineering Pro Street award. The reason behind the car's failure to sweep the podium as its older sibling had done three and four years prior remains somewhat controversial.

"I had built the J-2000 with the Competition Engineering *Pro Street Rulebook* literally hanging on the wall in the shop where I fabricated the car. I put every possible safety feature imaginable on the car and it should have scored out nearly perfect," he said. Initially the pizza cutter 3 1/2" Monocoque front wheels were shod with typical run-of-the-mill D.O.T. approved treads, while the gargantuan custom-made Firestone rear tires were not D.O.T. approved. However, with Competition Engineering, a division of Moroso, serving as the presenting sponsor of the pro street award, Dobbertin thought it might behoove him to swap on a set of the non-D.O.T. approved Moroso Front Runner tires. After all, the rules hadn't changed since Dobbertin's Nova—shod with non-D.O.T. approved McCreary back tires—won in '82 and '83. Plus, schmoozing the signature sponsor with their own product on the front wheels of the car couldn't be a bad thing, right?

Wrong.

A last-second rule change on the day of judging specified that non-D.O.T. approved tires resulted in a loss of ten points. Unfortunately for Rick, those ten points were the difference between first and second place, with Matt and Debbie Hay's 1984 Oldsmobile Ciera beating out the Poncho.

"Even if the rule change had been implemented on Friday night, twelve hours before the judging, I would have had plenty of time to swap the front tires and prevent the point loss," Dobbertin reflected. But by waiting until Saturday, judges left him no opportunity at all to address the rule switch.

Scuttlebutt soon began circulating that the rule change might have actually been more of a ploy to manipulate the points in order to spread the awards around so that the same car didn't win both Best Car and Best Pro Street Car at the same event.

Even Hay was surprised by the turn of events. "From a pure workmanship standpoint, it is the finest car I have ever seen," he acknowledged.[10] And while Hay's radical Ciera was a remarkable car in its own right, it had been debuted the year prior at the '85 Nationals where it won first place in the Best Street Machine category and second place in Pro Street. In the what-have-you-done-for-me-lately world of pro street cars, the fact that Dobbertin's incredible spankin' new build had been beaten out by a car that had already made a lap around the national show circuit was surprising to say the least.

Later, the J-2000 would be named 1986 Hot Rod of the Year,[14] one of *Hot Rod's* Top Ten Cars of the Decade (along with the Nova),[15] one of *Hot Rod's* Best Street Machines of All Time,[16] one of the Top 50 cars that helped define *Hot Rod*,[17] and one of the Best of the Decade by *Car Craft*. Additionally, Dobbertin brought the car back to Du Quoin in '87 where he fared better, winning Best Engine, Best Engineered, and the Competition Engineering Best Pro Street Award while taking second place behind Mark Grimes in Best Interior and Best Overall Street Machine.[18] Even as recently as June 2013, *Car Craft* revisited the car in a feature-length article.[19]

## Going Global: Part I

Not only was the J-2000 groundbreaking in terms of build quality and overall craftsmanship, it attained near rock-star status in the media. After two full-length features including the August 1986 cover of *Car Craft*, the Pontiac also graced the cover of the October 1986 issue of *Popular Hot Rodding* and was covered in detail in the same month's issue of *Hot Rod*, too.[6,7,9,10]

Dobbertin took some heat from his peers for appearing on the cover of *Car Craft* next to the car in a NASA jumpsuit with a J-2000-matching yellow airbrushed racing helmet in hand, but the incredible images created at GM Photographic by ace photographer Ed Sperko had elevated what we could all come to expect from a street machine magazine photo shoot.[7]

Also, a unique deal with Revell Model Corporation resulted in a 1:25 scale replica of the car being available in virtually every department store in the country. Dobbertin's J-2000 and later Matt & Debbie Hay's 1988 Thunderbird were made into quarter-scale kits so that any kid or would-be hot rodder could build their own version of the masterpieces. Additionally, the frame and engine parts of the Dobbertin kit were repackaged with Chevrolet Beretta and Corvette bodies and Hay's chassis was repackaged as a Lincoln, as well. In total, Revell released five pro street kits in the series.[20]

The initial plan was to release a new replica kit of one builder's car each year. Even though Dobbertin's J-2000 and Hay's Ford were both popular and sold relatively well, restructuring at Revell had cost project chief Bob Johnson his job.[20] With the J-2000 and T-bird already on the shelves and prototypes of Rocky Robertson's Buick already in the works, the project was scrapped.[20] Still popular with collectors, the kits are a tangible reminder of the widespread popularity of pro street that achieved all new heights with the construction of the J-2000.

The surprising second place Pro Street finish in '86 aside, Dobbertin's recollections of Du Quoin are overwhelmingly positive. "It was a gorgeous facility and really just a great place for the event," he said.[8] Like many of his contemporaries, Dobbertin says the stifling Southern Illinois heat and humidity is one of the things he remembers most. "It was always hot there, that's for sure," he added.

Dobbertin laughs heartily as he recalls one story from Du Quoin. Fellow pro street hero Scott Sullivan had a dead battery in his '55 Chevy and had asked Dobbertin for a jump. Gladly obliging, Dobbertin connected his half of the jumper cables to the J-2000 while Sullivan flashed his characteristic sly grin and quipped "Black to positive, right?"

"Even though he was obviously joking, when Scott said the words, his hands subconsciously actually connected black to positive," Dobbertin said. "So he hooks the jumper cables up backwards and blows my alternator right

there," he chuckled. "Here are two guys who obviously know a thing or two about cars and we can't even jump a dead battery. With a hundred people standing around, he looks at me and goes, 'Oops.'"

A blown alternator might seem bad, but it was a far cry from the narrowly averted disaster that could have befallen the J-2000 on a trip to Australia. Promoter Chic Henry had negotiated a deal with Dobbertin to get the Pontiac 'down under' for their first-ever 1988 Australian Summernats car show. Not only was the J-2000 the only car representing the United States, but in a unique twist, the car actually ended up leading one of the Australian bicentennial celebration parades through the capital city of Canberra. "I figured if the car was ever going to stop dead in its tracks or overheat, this would be the time—but it didn't miss a beat. It was a real honor to be part of such a prestigious event," Dobbertin recalled.

The J-2000 had been booked to appear at another show in Melbourne a of couple weeks later. On the morning of the trip south, Henry took his Ute (Australian utility vehicle) to a local shop to have the oil changed before towing the J-2000 to the show in his enclosed trailer. But apparently whoever changed the oil forgot to tighten the drain plug, so the oil soon found its way to the pavement.

The engine in the Ute blew before the J-2000's journey to Melbourne even began. Henry scrambled to acquire a rental so that the J-2000 could still be delivered on time and everything worked out just fine.

A couple weeks later, when Henry's Ute was up and running again, he drove to Melbourne to recover his trailer. Not too long into the trip home, a portion of the rear frame along with the tow hitch separated from the truck. As a result, the empty trailer broke free, careened out of control, landed in a ditch, and was nearly totaled. Had it not been for that faulty oil change, the J-2000 would have been aboard when the failure occurred, most assuredly resulting in its destruction, too. Thank goodness for some unnamed Australian's oil changing incompetence.

## chapter 4 | OVER THE TOP

### *Going Global: Part II*

Following up on the most decorated pro street car of the year is difficult. Doing it twice is next to impossible. After the monumental exertion and expenditure of time, talent, and resources to construct the Pontiac, Dobbertin opted to change course a bit and enjoy other pursuits. Many people might be content to let the stardom and notoriety garnered from two incredible street machines parlay over into business success building cars for others. But in case you hadn't surmised by now, Rick Dobbertin isn't like other people.

Heavily criticized for the impracticality of the J-2000, Dobbertin built a cool front-wheel drive pro street Pontiac Grand Am in 1988. A near 180-degree departure from his previous car, the Grand Am featured a stock drivetrain and interior with a mild tub job and some graphics. It was lightly covered in the media, but certainly didn't create the buzz to which Dobbertin had grown accustomed. The car is visible on the cover of both the October and November 1988 issues of *Car Craft* and was also briefly mentioned in *Hot Rod*, but was never fully featured.[21,22]

In 1991, Dobbertin spearheaded the effort to convert a bone-stock Ford pickup into a wild pro streeter in 55 hours on-site at the 1991 Street Machine Nationals.[23,24] Despite persistent rains all weekend, Dobbertin and his team of pro street heavy hitters including Wayne Bushey, Rich Gebhardt, Rocky Robertson, Kevin Rogers, Scott Sullivan, Danny Taylor, and many others started construction on the "Mild to Wild" project at 9 a.m. Friday morning and were done before the awards ceremony at 4 p.m. on Sunday. In a world before reality television, it was an impressive display of collaboration under pressure, with the end result being a pretty trick truck.[23,24]

From there, Dobbertin's story turns from remarkable to bizarre. He built a sea-worthy 32-foot long amphibious vehicle out of an old stainless steel milk tanker. Initially intended to circumnavigate the globe, The Dobbertin Surface Orbiter (DSO) was yet another incredible piece of craftsmanship and engineering from the hands of a man who, after all, had no formal engineering training and was a self-taught fabricator. Dobbertin and his

wife at the time lived aboard the vessel for nearly three years throughout a 28-country, 38-state trek that covered 30,000 miles on land and 3,000 miles at sea, including a passage through the Panama Canal.[25] Dobbertin's exploits aboard the DSO were nothing short of remarkable and certainly worthy of a book all their own.

In 2002, Dobbertin turned his talents and attention to building a high performance amphibious vehicle that ultimately resulted in the construction of the Dobbertin HydroCar (DHC). Initially intended to run 125+ mph on land and 60+ mph on water, the innovative machine has proven the most challenging test yet of the talented designer and fabricator's ingenuity. Although the HydroCar was never featured in any of the major automotive publications, it did land the cover spot on the January 2004 *Popular Mechanics,* along with a feature article titled "Surf 'N Turf."[26]

Dobbertin is content with his place in street machine history. He nearly ended up placing both of his cars on *Hot Rod's* "Ten Best Street Machines of All Time," a feat only accomplished by Sullivan, but ultimately the Nova just missed the cut. His J-2000 has become the barometer by which every other pro street car is compared and thus far, some 27 years later, no car has even come close. And as so many have said, whether you love it or hate it, there is simply no denying the masterful, obsessive craftsmanship necessary to pull it off.

In a way, the 1986 Street Machine Nationals owe a great deal to the legendary pro street builders of the era. After all, the show had worn out its welcome in three different towns already and roared into Du Quoin with one heck of a reputation. Thanks to an incredible collection of more than 3000 of the finest street machines in the land, that reputation rapidly pivoted from one of excessive consumption of alcohol to yet another of outrageous displays of awesomeness. And for most folks, none of those thousands of cars were more outrageous or awesome than the heavily articulated and highly decorated creation of Rick Dobbertin.

## References

1. Garson P. Radical Roots. *Car Craft*. March 1987:89-96, 127.
2. Hanson C. Prince of Pro Street. *Car Craft*. February 1984:62-67..
3. Baskerville G. Overkill. *Hot Rod*. September 1982:70-73.
4. Dafur T. And the Winner Is... *Car Craft*. October 1982:76-79.
5. Hall A. Nova To Go, With Everything. *Popular Hot Rodding*. October 1982:46-48.
6. Hampson B. One Step Beyond: Part 2. *Car Craft*. September 1986:115-121.
7. Hampson B. One Step Beyond: Part I. *Car Craft*. August 1986:24-30.
8. Dobbertin R. Custom car builder. Personal communication: Telephone interview. May 17, 2011.
9. Tann J. Top Gun. *Popular Hot Rodding*. October 1986:30-33, 90.
10. Baskerville G. Out Radical Rageous. *Hot Rod*. October 1986:32-36.
11. Whittington C. Custom painter. Personal communication: Telephone interview. March 24, 2013.
12. Freiburger D. Top 100 Hot Rods That Changed the World. *Hot Rod*. February 2009.
13. Smith J. Automotive journalist, former editor of Car Craft and Hot Rod. Personal communication: Telephone interview. May 12, 2011.
14. Baskerville G. Hot Rod Magazine's Top Ten. *Hot Rod*. December 1986:22-25.
15. Baechtel J. Top Ten Cars of the Decade. *Hot Rod*. December 1989:41-46.
16. Kinnan R. The Ten Best Street Machines of All Time. *Hot Rod*. August 1995:20-27.
17. Smith J. Fifty Fabulous Features. *Hot Rod*. August 1998:96.
18. Bernsau T. Street Machine Nationals. *Car Craft*. October 1987:32-45.

19. Smith J. Dobbertin's J2000: The Car That Changed It All. *Car Craft*. June 2013:76-80.
20. Sexton E. Project Manager, Revell, Inc. Personal communication: Telephone interview. June 10, 2011.
21. Smith J. Dobbertin Builds Front-Wheel-Drive Pro Street Car. *Hot Rod*. August 1988:20.
22. Hatano B. Kings of Pro Street. *Car Craft*. November 1988:18-28.
23. Bernsau T. *The Best of the Street Machine Nationals, 1972-1993*. Los Angeles, CA: Petersen Publishing Company; 1993.
24. Bernsau T. Street Machine Nationals. *Car Craft*. October 1991:18-31.
25. Dobbertin R. Rick Dobbertin Bio. http://www.dobbertinhydrocar.com. Accessed May 17, 2011.
26. Gromer C. Surf 'N Turf. *Popular Mechanics*. January 2004:62-67.

# chapter 5

# LOVIN' EVERY MINUTE OF IT
## 1980-1985

# chapter 5 | LOVIN' EVERY MINUTE OF IT: 1980-1985

*I'm not man or machine*
*I'm just something in between*
*(Whoa-oa-whoa-oh-whoa)*
*I'm all love, a dynamo*
*So push the button and let me go*
*(Whoa-oa-whoa-oh-whoa)*
*You want me to come alive*
*Just flick the switch into overdrive*
*You and me can let it be*
*Ready-Aim-Fire*

*Touch that dial-Turn me on*
*Start me like a motor, Make me run*

*Lovin' every minute of it*

"Lovin' Every Minute of It," by Robert "Mutt" Lange; © copyright 1985, Universal Music Publishing Corp.[1]

## Party on Wheels

By 1980, the Street Machine Nationals had grown from a car show that organizers hoped would be successful into a full-blown nationwide phenomenon. The encouraging turnout of 1,300+ cars and 10,000 spectators in year one had ballooned into 5,000 cars and around 30,000 spectators for the show's fourth installment in 1980.[2] Event management, still composed of

*Car Craft* staffers, recognized the necessity of capping the car count at 5,000 cars simply because the facility in Indianapolis could not safely accommodate more. Although no one ever kept count, cars turned away after the cap likely numbered in the thousands.[3]

Wisely, Petersen execs recognized the opportunity to accommodate more cars and broaden the appeal of the already red-hot Street Machine Nationals brand. The first spin-off show, the 1979 Street Machine Nationals West, was held in Pomona, California in October and moved to Northridge for 1980. The event was a modest success but quaint by Nationals standards, averaging just over 800 cars and 10,000 spectators.

The small size of the West show would probably be a surprise to most *CC* readers, as the magazine devoted seven pages of coverage to the Nats West in 1979 and eight pages in 1980, including full color spreads both years.[4,5] By comparison, the big show in Indy got just one more page than the West show had received in 1979, while the 1980 Indy show got five additional pages.[2,6] The magazine began to recognize that coverage in print could be a powerful force to grow an event. Properly staged and purposefully photographed, even a weak show could be made to look like a huge gathering.

While the "big show" had grown and seemed vibrant and healthy by all outward appearances, all wasn't perfect back in Indianapolis. The 1979 event had neared the 5,000 car capacity and event planners fully expected to hit the cap for 1980. Law enforcement officials had easily handled the show for the first two go-'rounds, as the crowd size was paltry compared to other events in the city such as the Indianapolis Marathon and the Indy 500.[3]

However, by 1979, the crowd was sizable and growing increasingly rowdy.[3] Revelers seemed more interested in partying than anything else. *Car Craft* editor Jon Asher recognized the swelling negative sentiment toward the event in the minds of Indy-area law officials and residents and decided to address the situation in the May issue of the magazine.

"As exciting as the Nationals are, the one aspect of last year's event that simply cannot be repeated under any circumstances is the on-the-streets burnouts that lead to arrests and very unfavorable nationwide publicity," Asher wrote.[7] In what would become a recognizable trend at the Nats, Asher also recognized that at least a portion of the growing negative element of the event was not comprised of participants or even spectators. He felt most of the problems could be traced to locals who thought the event was a great excuse to get a little crazy, and they were "lovin' every minute of it."

The legal risk was a grave concern for Petersen Publishing, whose *Car Craft* name on the show exposed them to a very real threat of liability should something go wrong. Eventually such concerns would lead Petersen to remove the *Car Craft* name altogether. To make matters worse, officials in Indy were threatening to pull the plug on hosting the event if things didn't change in a hurry for the 1980 show.[3,7]

Locals weren't the only ones to blame for the growing problems. Show founder Harry Hibler recognized that a number of participants were misbehaving, too. "You've got to remember, these were a bunch of young enthusiasts who had a lot of horsepower under the hood, and they were gonna get out and show off," Hibler said.[3] "We tried to control them as tightly as possible and keep them on the grounds with all types of entertainment stuff and keep them off the street, but when they got away from that they let loose," he added.

That "letting loose" posed a very real threat to bystanders who could potentially be in the path of a burnout-gone-wrong, not to mention the overwhelming sound and smell of thousands of street machines striking tires in the streets. To a growing number of residents, the show had become an unwanted nuisance.

"We vexed the local authorities. As much as they liked it and wanted the revenue, they had townspeople who would say that they didn't want the event there and pressure them to get rid of it," Hibler added. Although the number of people who voiced concerns paled in comparison to the number of show proponents who usually did not thank or otherwise approach their civic leaders, that voice of dissent began to trigger some in Indianapolis to consider if it was all really worth the hassle. By 1981, the relationship had seriously begun to sour and Car Craft officials were actively courting another spot for the event.

Despite mounting concerns about the location of the event, the show itself continued to grow and the build quality of the cars that appeared year after year had significantly improved. One of those cars, Scott Sullivan's '67 Nova, had premiered the year before with little fanfare except from magazine types with cameras in hand. After seeing the car in all three major publications in '79, spectators flocked to get a first-hand glimpse of the car in 1980.

"It was insane," recounted Sullivan. "I pull in the fairgrounds in Indy and you would have thought I was a rock star. People were running and screaming 'There's the car!' Camera flashes were going off all around me. I was afraid I was going to run somebody over," he recalled. "What was craziest was that it was pretty much the same car from the year before when nobody had really seemed to even notice it."[8]

Perhaps on account of Sullivan and other pioneers like Steve Lisk and Gary Kollofski, the popularity of pro street continued to grow. Recognizing this growth and poised to capitalize on it, chassis component manufacturer Competition Engineering signed on to sponsor the first-ever professionally judged pro street competition in 1980. The brainchild of CE president Fred Gerle, the award would eventually become one of the most coveted honors at the Nationals.[9] Joe Burek's Boss 302 Ford Maverick beat out Sullivan's Nova for first place.[9]

### You Don't Have to Go Home, But You Can't Stay Here

1981 would mark the last year of the show in Indianapolis. Although the Street Machine Nationals franchise expanded again, adding a Northern California event in addition to the West show and the original "big show," Petersen execs and Indianapolis city fathers were both obviously in I-think-it's-time-we-see-other-people mode. The question was no longer *would* the show move but *where* would it end up.

"We had kind of dis-invited ourselves from Indy," recounted former *CC* editor Jeff Smith. "The problem with the Nationals was that you had 5,000 cars all in a small area. We tried to clamp down on it during the day

## chapter 5 | LOVIN' EVERY MINUTE OF IT: 1980-1985

because the minute you let someone get away with a burnout or something, it just gets crazy," he shared. And just as Hibler pointed out, Smith felt that the problem was never really inside the event but rather outside on the streets after the gates to the fairgrounds were closed.

By Nats standards, 1981 was a ho-hum kind of year. A quick look through magazine coverage and interviews with attendees reveals that, unlike other years, there were really no new newsworthy cars to speak of. On the other hand, participant count stayed at a busting-at-the-seams 5,000 cars and spectator count was over 60,000.[9,10] The real news was where the show would end up for 1982.

Before that decision was made, another switch that would eventually have far-reaching implications for Du Quoin and the Street Machine Nationals occurred in the *Car Craft* offices. Show originator and *CC* Executive Editor Harry Hibler took over at *Hot Rod* and former editor John Dianna took Hibler's spot.[11] It would eventually be Dianna's call to pull all magazine coverage for the show—the move that would eventually strangle the Nats and contribute to their demise.[12]

### *Off to the Land of Lincoln*

Lee Lasky, hired in 1980 at Petersen as Special Events Director, worked hard to strike the deal that would move the show 200 miles due-east to Springfield, Illinois for 1982.[13] Negotiations weren't without their difficulties, though. Indy's local media coverage of the event in 1981 was brutal.

*CC* Editor Jon Asher referred to most of the bad ink as "more than just exaggerations." In fact, Asher contended that the reports were "completely ludicrous."[13] Whether they were true or not, Lasky had to perform quite a sales job in order to get leaders in Springfield to sign on, but managed to do so in time for the announcement in the February issue.[14]

The change in address sure didn't do anything to dampen enthusiasm for the show. All 5,000 available spots were accounted for in just a week after entry blanks were made available in the February '82 *CC*.[9]

Some would-be participants were getting wise to the fact that registration filled quickly. They attempted some creative tactics to be sure and secure a spot. Rules specified that no copied entry forms from 1981 would be accepted and that no submissions postmarked before January 12 would be allowed, either.[14] A total of 761 participants decided it was best to avoid trusting the US Postal Service at all, opting instead for Fed Ex, Purolator, Airborne Express, Emery Air Freight, and hand delivery to be sure they'd get a place.[15]

As exciting as the fast-filling registration process had been, Asher's June editorial belied a simmering concern that unless the hard partying, law-breaking reputation the event had earned wasn't stomped down quickly, its future was in serious jeopardy.

"We're literally all in this together," he wrote. "We could just as easily be out of it together. I, for one, am hoping that there'll be a Street Machine Nationals to go to for a lot of years to come," he added.[13] Little did he know that by 1986 the Nats would be rolling into their fourth home in six years and Springfield would give them the boot after just three events.

The '82 show proved to be a smashing success. Headlined by Rick Dobbertin's awesome 1965 blown and twin turbocharged Nova, the real trophy fight was for second place, as no other ride came close.[16,17] With 5,000 cars (again) and more than 75,000 spectators, turnout in Springfield had surpassed Indy by at least 15,000 bodies.[16] Any concerns about moving the show from its birthplace were quickly put to rest.

With careful planning and crossed fingers, Springfield law enforcement and city officials alike escaped 1982 without serious incident. Hopes were high that 1983 would cement Springfield as the new home of the Nationals. Registration for the event filled in less than two days.[9]

Asher extolled the community of Springfield and their love for the event in the pages of the magazine. "It is backed by a 100 percent cooperative community that's a joy to work with. From the politicians to the police to the press, Springfield is a dynamite town," he wrote.[18]

Apparently the love fest wasn't mutual. Sixteen months later, Springfield insisted on evicting the Nats, leaving them homeless again.

Back on the fairgrounds, '83 would again be domination by Dobbertin, and more than 100,000 spectators were on hand to witness the spectacle.[19] Rick's radical Nova was back and unchanged but still managed to haul off pretty much every trophy up for grabs. The back-to-back sweep proved that the car really was so far ahead of its time that no one else had caught up even though they'd been given a full year.

Soon-to-be-familiar names like Rod Saboury, Matt Hay, Rick Dyer, and Danny Taylor began to pop up on the awards sheet in 1983. Saboury's nasty blown, injected, and tubbed '69 Camaro made the cover and snagged a full color feature in the October '83 issue of *CC*, a fact worth mentioning if only for the fact that it was not a Saboury-trademark Corvette.[19,20] Saboury would go on to build five different featured 'Vettes, but the Camaro was his first car featured in a magazine.

Elsewhere, Petersen execs decided that the 1982 show schedule of one event in the Midwest and two in California needed to be tweaked a bit in order to better spread the SM Nats brand, so the NorCal show was scrapped and a new Street Machine Nationals East show was added.[21] Hosted at the New York State Fairgrounds, it too was a relatively lightly attended affair reserved primarily for locals and procrastinators who missed the deadline for the Big Dance in Springfield.

## *Leaving So Soon?*

1984 would prove to be the final year in Springfield. In what would soon become SM Nats tradition, the triple-digit Illinois heat and 97% humidity was stifling. It wasn't enough to scare away a new record crowd, though. More than 113,000 onlookers in various shades of necessitated or premeditated undress came to witness what *CC* staffer Bruce Hampson dubbed "The Greatest Show on Earth."[22]

Petersen Publications had established the Street Machine Nationals into the premiere late-model street machine spectacular over the course of eight years. However, all those efforts were essentially wiped out by a few knuckleheads doing burnouts and generally causing trouble for just a few

hours late Saturday night during the event. *CC* Editor Jeff Smith was stern but accurate in his October '84 "Point of View" in the aftermath of the debacle.

"The Street Machine Nationals are in trouble," he wrote. "*Car Craft* and the Street Machine Nationals will not return to Springfield next year," he added.[23] Apparently a throng had gathered for an impromptu tire roasting at a strip mall, while other similar exhibitions in motel parking lots across the city had resulted in countless arrests and citations.[24] Springfield decided they had had enough.

Tim Farley, Executive Director of the Springfield Convention and Visitor's Bureau for the past 21 years, lived near the Springfield facility as a child and remembers the show well. "It was very exciting for the community, but after a while it became very *hazardous* to the community," he said.[24] After a truck flipped and the driver and occupants were seriously injured, local policymakers faced the stark truth that regardless of the economic impact of the show, the combination of high horsepower, 100,000+ people, and free-flowing booze was a potentially deadly mix.

Following the ouster from Springfield, the Nats were a valuable but troubled free agent. The money and recognition the show could bring to any community willing to give it a go was significant and all but guaranteed. After all, 113,000 people coming into town needed food, lodging, fuel, and—in the case of the Nats crowd—at least a case or two of beer and a couple of gallons of burnout bleach. The buying power of such a crowd was tremendous. Depending on who you ask, economic impact estimates ranged from anywhere between $1 million[24] to as much as $16.5 million.[25]

But when civic leaders pulled out their pencils and calculators and really did the math, they started to realize that the added expense of law enforcement and the physical and psychological toll the show could inflict on their towns usually overshadowed the potential profits. As a result, most places that had the facilities necessary to host the event wanted no part of it.

## Gateway to the Worst

The show managed to land in East St. Louis at St. Louis International Raceway (now Gateway International Raceway) for a one-year engagement in 1985. Special Events Founder and CEO Bruce Hubley, whose organization had been involved with the marketing and promotion of the show since its second year in 1978, remembers the difficulty in hosting that '85 show all too well.

"We landed in this rather difficult situation in St. Louis," he said. "From an operations standpoint, it was a bad move," Hubley revealed. The show was a logistical nightmare, with only one way in and one way out of the isolated drag strip complex. With temperatures again in the triple digits, absolutely no shade in sight, and traffic snarled for hours at a time, nerves frayed and tempers flared. Fights broke out and police in riot gear armed with tear gas and trained dogs were on high alert.[26] Stuff was getting real.

Publishing magnate Robert Petersen's personal attorney Robert Gottlieb attended the event and walked away aghast at what he thought was a significant legal risk to the company and to Petersen personally. In light of all the negative press, Hubley saw his opportunity to purchase the much-maligned custom car exhibition franchise. He approached Petersen President Fred Waingrow and offered to buy the event.

Waingrow agreed. A deal was struck for all Petersen shows including the Car Craft Street Machine Nationals, the Hot Rod Supernationals, and the Four Wheel & Off-Road Four Wheel Jamboree. Upon signing the contract, Hubley took ownership and all magazine names were immediately dropped from event titles.[27]

Deep in the fine print of the new agreement was the fact that although Hubley's operation would own and produce the shows, Petersen magazines would still provide editorial coverage. This allowed *Car Craft*, *Hot Rod*, and *Four Wheel & Off-Road* to continue to enjoy the benefits of the feature content the shows generated for their respective titles without the significant legal risk associated with hosting them. In return, Special

Events would retain any profits from operating the events while still getting the added benefit of the magazine coverage so critical in marketing the shows nationwide.

Meanwhile amid the pepper spray and German Shepherds, several new cars were debuted that wowed the crowds. Matt & Debbie Hay proved they were major players and kicked off a new trend by tricking out a late-model car. Their alcohol-burning blown and injected 1984 Oldsmobile was the hit of the show, snagging first place in the Best Street Machine category.[28] Other notables at the event included Steve Williams' Sullivan-built '66 Chevelle, Rocky Robertson's '69 Nova, and Rich Gebhardt's first feature car, a 1982 Monte Carlo.[28] Future street hero and Ridetech Founder Bret Voelkel's clean yellow Mustang fastback graced the cover of the October '85 *CC* that detailed the event.

You couldn't have predicted that the show was in trouble just by reading the magazine. Event coverage for that problematic 1985 show largely sidestepped the issues that had surfaced. In his October '85 editorial, *CC* Editor Jeff Smith gave passing mention to the fact that the show would again be moving but was short on details.[29] Behind the scenes, he and Hubley were working feverishly to find a suitable location for 1986.

"In my mind, 1985 was the worst year of the Street Machine Nationals," he said. The longtime promoter and successful businessman says he never for a moment considered hosting the event in East St. Louis again.[27]

Smith agreed. "It was just a horrible show. It just didn't go well and we knew we couldn't go back there," he said.[26]

Moving it to a new location was top priority, and after a few short months of vetting and negotiations, Ionia, Michigan, agreed to host the 1986 Street Machine Nationals.[30]

That is, until they decided not to.

## chapter 5 | LOVIN' EVERY MINUTE OF IT: 1980-1985

## *References*

1. Lovin' Every Minute of It. 2013; http://www.lyricsfreak.com/l/loverboy/lovin+every+minute+of+it_20085558.html. Accessed March 15, 2013.
2. Smith J. Indy '80. *Car Craft*. October 1980:50-63; 86-87.
3. Hibler H. Former publisher, Hot Rod Magazine. Personal communication: Telephone interview. May 25, 2011.
4. Smith J. The Wild Wild West: Street Machine Nationals. *Car Craft*. February 1980:22-27; 95.
5. Smith J. Vanity Fair: The 1980 Street Machine Nationals West. *Car Craft*. February 1981:64-71.
6. Smith J, Asher J, Britt N. Supercar Summer. *Car Craft*. October 1979:26-33.
7. Asher J. Don't Read This Unless You Care About the Street Machine Nationals. *Car Craft*. May 1980:4-6.
8. Sullivan S. Custom car builder. Personal communication: Telephone interview. May 18, 2011.
9. Bernsau T. *The Best of the Street Machine Nationals, 1972-1993*. Los Angeles, CA: Petersen Publishing Company; 1993.
10. Mayersohn N. The Indy 5000. *Car Craft*. October 1981:24-32.
11. Asher J. The Changing of the Guard. *Car Craft*. February 1982:4.
12. Schifsky C. Former Editor, Car Craft. Personal communication: Telephone interview. May 27, 2011.
13. Asher J. The Street Machine Nationals and You. *Car Craft*. June 1982:4.
14. Asher J. First Chance to Enter! *Car Craft*. February 1982:21-22.
15. Asher J. Enthusiasm and the Common Car Crafter. *Car Craft*. April 1982:5.
16. Dafur T. Springfield Follies. *Car Craft*. October 1982:20-30.
17. Dafur T. And the Winner Is... *Car Craft*. October 1982:76-79.
18. Asher J. The Nationals Are Coming! The Nationals Are Coming! *Car Craft*. March 1983:2,112.

19. Hanson C. Hotter Than Ever. *Car Craft*. October 1983:28-43; 105.
20. Asher J. The Changeling. *Car Craft*. October 1983:100-103.
21. Smith J. New York! New York! *Car Craft*. July 1983:47.
22. Hampson B. The Greatest Show on Earth. *Car Craft*. October 1984:64.
23. Smith J. Where Do We Go From Here? *Car Craft*. October 1984:5.
24. Farley T. Executive Director, Springfield Convention & Business Center. Personal communication: Telephone interview. May 20, 2011.
25. Family Events. 22nd Annual Street Machine Nationals. Internal report. June 15 1998.
26. Smith J. Automotive journalist, former editor of Car Craft and Hot Rod. Personal communication: Telephone interview. May 12, 2011.
27. Hubley B. Founder and CEO of Family Events, Inc. Personal communication: Telephone interview. May 22, 2012.
28. Boales K. Street Machine Nationals. *Car Craft*. October 1985:18-26.
29. Smith J. The Ultimate Cruise. *Car Craft*. October 1985:4.
30. Smith J. National Report. *Car Craft*. March 1986:101-102.

# chapter 6

# THE HAY TEAM
## MATT & DEBBIE HAY

## chapter 6 | THE HAY TEAM

### *Oh My Goshen, She's Pretty!*

**M**att Hay grew up a typical Midwest kid. Like many youngsters in his hometown of Goshen, Indiana, he spent his days building model cars, bicycles, and eventually autos. Basically if it had wheels, it was a target for customization by the future pro street hero.

Fueled by a steady stream of ideas lifted from car magazines, his young mind was always scheming up ways to make his stuff faster, cooler, or both. As a precocious fourth grade fabricator, he managed to stretch the forks on his Schwinn Stingray. He was undoubtedly the baddest and most talented builder in his loosely formed elementary school "bike gang."[1]

As Matt matured, his attention turned to two things: cars and girls. In a formula as old as time, young Hay had it all figured out: get the cool car first, then leverage it to lure in the cute girl second. His first target would be a '66 Mustang. His second would be a cute brunette named Deb.

Without all the distractions of big city life, Matt says his love for cars most likely stemmed from the fact that customizing and cruising cars was about all that was happening in Goshen.[2] "I was a little bit into cars in high

school like all guys," he said. "I didn't go into college immediately, so I started tinkering with an old Mustang that I had. That's where it all started—I couldn't leave well enough alone," he added.

Hay had purchased the 'Stang used for $400 in 1973 at the age of sixteen. Later, he decided to horrify the Ford purists in his hometown by transplanting a blown small block Chevy into the car. Hay says the main reason he attempted the swap was just to prove to himself that he could.

One night in 1977 while cruising in his faithful steed, he happened to notice a pretty girl in a sparkling new El Camino sitting outside the Burger Chef. After a couple of quick squirts of Binaca and a brief moment to summon his courage, he approached. The rest, as they say, is history.

The details of that history, however, are the stuff of pro street legend. A series of four magazine-caliber cars of progressively improved build quality, refinement, and complexity would eventually roll out of the Hays' typical household garage.

The first—that very same '66 Ford—was featured along with a handful of other cars in the November '78 issue of *Hot Rod* shortly after the second annual Street Machine Nationals in Indy.[3] By '79, Matt had treated the car to a full back half and tub job. The changes were enough to land the car in print again, this time in the October 1979 issue of *Popular Hot Rodding,* just one page away from Sullivan's '67 Nova.[4]

After turning their attention to domestic pursuits and marrying in 1980, The Dynamic Duo of Pro Street came back with an even stronger effort in 1983. Their low-slung 1979 Mustang took second place behind Dobbertin's Nova for Best Car at the '83 Nationals in Springfield.[5] Again fitted with a blown small block Chevy, the car featured a full Alston tube chassis and an incredible slammed stance.

Although it was a completely different car from the '66, the titles of both features were exactly the same. It seemed the folks at *Popular Hot Rodding* were struggling with creativity a bit, dubbing both the Hays' Mustangs "Halfbreed" in reference to the small block Chevy propulsion in the Fords.[4,6]

Although the Hays had purchased the '79 Mustang brand new, it would be nearly three years until Matt worked up enough bravery to take a torch to the shiny new pony for the sake of street machine greatness.[6,7] The well-built creation was the result of a true team effort using what Matt describes as nothing more than simple hand tools in a modest two-car garage. In fact, the creative team even used the garage *as* a tool, employing the garage door as a sheet metal brake to shape some of the hand-crafted tinwork in the car.[2]

## *Raising the Bar*

With two magazine covers, four full-color features, and a respectable showing at the greatest gathering of street machines in the world by the end of 1983, the couple was hungry for more. At the same time, they had left Indiana in the rearview mirror, relocating to Chandler, Arizona, in 1984.

In an unprecedented move that would light the wick on a hot new trend for well over a decade, Matt selected a brand new front-wheel-drive car for use as a starting point for his next project. A sleepy-looking refrigerator white Oldsmobile Ciera was purchased fresh off the lot, taken home, and completely disassembled. It would be built back from the ground up in radical pro street trim.

"The Olds was a family car and—again—I just wanted to prove to myself that I could do it and make it look halfway decent," he said with a chuckle.[2] The new Olds stole the show at the Nationals in East St. Louis in 1985. Soon-to-be fellow pro street legend Rocky Robertson remembered it well.

"There were lots of cool cars there in 1985, but Matt's Olds was all I cared about," he said. "A new car that also wasn't a Chevy? It was groundbreaking," he added.[8] The Ciera was a cool corporate cousin to the Buick Somerset Robertson would debut just a year later.

Far more radical than either Mustang, the Oldsmobile sported a wicked alcohol-burning blown and injected small block and a full Alston tube chassis.[9] Once again, the pair had built a car that took the cover on two different magazines, landing the November '85 issue of *Hot Rod* and the June '86 issue of *Car Craft*, making *Hot Rod*'s prestigious Top Ten for '85.[9,10]

With freshened "heartbeat" style graphics for 1986, the car narrowly beat out Dobbertin's J-2000 for the Competition Engineering Pro Street

award in Du Quoin.[11] Although it looked awesome, the thirsty small block got just 1.8 miles per gallon. Coupled with its eight-gallon fuel cell, the Olds wasn't exactly a great candidate for a trip that extended much beyond the end of the block. The *Hot Rod* feature—written before Matt had really had a chance to fully sort the car—had a particularly harsh tone, suggesting the car was not a legitimate street machine. Streetable or not, it was still an impressive piece of craftsmanship. And more importantly, it just looked *nasty*.

Jeff Smith recalled one story attached to the car. "We had lined up Paul Martinez, a freelance photographer in the Phoenix area, to shoot the car along with Warren Johnson's pro stocker," he said. "The day we were shooting it, we got word that the Challenger Shuttle had exploded. It put a bit of a pall over the whole thing," he added somberly.[12]

Unfortunately for Matt and all the rest of his pro street fraternity mates, building a successful car usually meant that the only question people would ask was what you planned to build next. At a cost of over $40,000 not including labor, the Oldsmobile represented a modern-day investment of over $87,000 in parts alone.[10] However, after two years on the show circuit, most people treated the car like yesterday's news.[2]

## *Thunderstruck*

Following the smashing success of the Ciera, Ford marketing representatives approached the couple in 1987 with an intriguing offer. Company execs wanted to promote the newly redesigned Thunderbird and the hot-off-the-presses Thunderbird Turbo Coupe. Recognizing that whatever the Hays built would get tons of press, Ford offered to send a roller factory test car out to Arizona for free in exchange for the positive ink the car would surely receive.

The Hays proved them right. Within a year, their newest creation would not only be featured in all three major magazines (including three covers), it would also do extremely well on the show circuit. Additionally, like Dobbertin's J-2000, it was also made into a new Revell model kit. Not bad press for Ford for the cost of a used body shell.

chapter 6 | THE HAY TEAM

The deal also added a level of legitimacy to the project that opened the floodgates for other smaller marketing sponsorships. "Once we got the deal from Ford, tons of other people jumped aboard to help out," Matt recalled. "I still had quite a bit of money invested out of pocket including all the labor, but the car probably wouldn't have been possible without the support of places like B&M, Alston, Mickey Thompson, Centerline, and so many others," he added.

Once finished, the car was a breathtaking piece of machinery. It featured a twin supercharged 351 engine with a scratch-built front-mounted induction system. The screaming neon pink paint with silver graphics was good enough for first place at the '88 SM Nats. In one of the most competitive years ever at the Nationals, Matt and Debbie also walked away with the CE Pro Street Award, took second place in the best supercharged vehicle category behind Mark Grimes' *triple* supercharged Eurosport, and were named runner-up for Best Overall Street Machine.[13]

Just like their previous three cars, the Hays' T-Bird was built almost entirely out of their now three-car attached garage at their home in Phoenix. "You did what you could to get things done," Hay recounted. While Alan Root handled engine-building duty on the Thunderbird, the wild and creative front-mounted twin supercharger system was entirely Matt's design. He mocked up the entire system using wood, then scratch-built the parts from aluminum.[14,15] The end result was stunning.

*Popular Hot Rodding* immediately named the car to its list of 10 Best Pro Street Cars Ever Built.[16] *Hot Rod* selected it to their annual Top Ten list.[17] However, just like the Oldsmobile before it, some magazine coverage was again critical of the street practicality as well as the strip functionality of the Hays' beautiful new machine. Immediately following the 1988 Street Machine Nationals, *Car Craft* had organized a small exhibition for a few cars and builders at I-57 Dragway, a nearby 1/8 strip in Benton, Illinois.[18] The colorful 'Bird's lackluster performance didn't do much to dispel the notion that the high-dollar fairgrounds cruisers were all show and no go.

The car was so new at the time of testing, Matt says he hadn't even had time to drive it around the block before loading up and making the 1,600+

mile trip to Du Quoin. The car initially sported Mikuni sidedraft carburetors, but once Hay got home and had a chance to install a direct port fuel injection system, its performance was much improved. "It was a SCREAMER and very drivable after we put the EFI on it," Hay said.

Unlike most builders whose wives are rarely mentioned in features let alone involved in the build, Matt insists that construction on each of their cars was a shared experience. "Every one of our cars was a team effort. Deb really put a lot of time in and she was involved 100%," he acknowledged. The only show Debbie ever missed during the couple's years on the circuit was at the Nationals in Du Quoin in 1986. The mother-to-be was great with child, expecting to deliver within the next month. She and Matt decided it was probably best for her to stay home and avoid the scorching heat and long days on her feet roaming the fairgrounds.

Matt is quick to point out the fact that year in and year out, the Du Quoin show was always a good time. "Compared to Indianapolis and Springfield, it was a great place," he said. "It was huge, but more than the facility, what I really remember most were the friends. Scott (Sullivan), Rick (Dobbertin), and everybody else just made that whole time special. It was like a family reunion every summer," he concluded.[2]

## Life After Pro Street

Years of hard work, long travel, and countless show dates had left the Hays ready for a breather after the buzz surrounding the Thunderbird died down. The emotional, physical, and financial drain of being a respected builder, functioning at the highest level of the sport for the better part of a decade, was intense. At the same time, the seemingly premeditated movement away from pro street by all the major magazines left the pair feeling somewhat used and abused.

"I got out for several reasons. Our family was growing, but more than that, at the time everything got real political," he revealed. "The major magazines started dictating what they wanted with illustrations and saying that everyone needed to get back to building stuff you could drive on the street," he said. But by Hay's way of thinking, he built his cars with a vision and hoped the masses would enjoy them.

"It was kind of the end and we just got fed up," he added. The Hays briefly considered opening their own shop and Matt actually built a wild 1949 Mercury for the same individual who purchased the Thunderbird. The Merc featured a radical Hemi and a unique articulated body. However, it became pretty clear early in the process that owning a high-end custom shop would most likely be an unwise decision.

"When we built our own cars, I loved just about every second of it," he said. "But I've got to tell you, I absolutely *hated* just about every second of building a car for somebody else where I didn't feel like I had the freedom to make all the decisions," he added. Stifled by the lack of creative license he had enjoyed turning wrenches on his own stuff, Matt wisely chose to keep his day job with a truck and van conversion company.

In 1999, Matt opted to start his own business buying and selling Indy cars and parts, a venture still in operation today. Meanwhile, Debbie became a children's minister and currently serves at City of Grace in Mesa. The couple still resides in Chandler and has toyed with the idea of reacquiring and restoring one of their old builds for nostalgia's sake.

The Hays complement one another well. For most guys, a wife who would just be willing to allow an automotive toy or two without nagging or complaining would be a dream come true. For Matt Hay, not only was his beloved willing to allow him to follow his dreams, she actually encouraged it. To top that, after encouraging it, she helped him *build* it. Then to top *that* she did it *again* three more times with progressively more involved and expensive builds each time. It is all just a part of what makes the couple's relationship so special.

In the Street Machine Nationals world of hard partying and fast cars, it is safe to say that a husband and wife duo is rare. What is more, the behavior of some showgoers was downright hostile to women. However, much like their cars, the Hays always seemed to emerge with class and style. It is no stretch to say the Street Machine Nationals were a better place because they were involved.

    The only question that remains unanswered after all these years is whether it was Matt's clever wit, rugged good looks, minty fresh breath, or his tricked out '66 Mustang that proved irresistible on that fateful Friday night in 1977. Only one woman knows for sure and she was unavailable for comment.

    It seems she's out in the garage.

## References

1. Garson P. Radical Roots. *Car Craft.* March 1987:89-96, 127.
2. Hay M. Custom car builder. Personal communication: Telephone interview. May 12, 2012.
3. Baskerville G. The Wild Bunch. *Hot Rod.* November 1978:26-31.
4. Emanuelson L. Halfbreed. *Popular Hot Rodding.* October 1979:58.
5. Hanson C. Hotter Than Ever. *Car Craft.* October 1983:28-43; 105.
6. Benty C. Halfbreed. *Popular Hot Rodding.* November 1983:42-44.
7. Asher J. Haulin' Oats. *Car Craft.* February 1984:16-19.
8. Robertson R. Custom car builder. Personal communication: Telephone interview. March 12, 2012.
9. Ganahl P. Pro Street: Who's Kidding Who? *Hot Rod.* November 1985:17-22.
10. Boales K. Vision Quest. *Car Craft.* June 1986:22-31.
11. Smith J. National Report. *Car Craft.* March 1986:101-102.
12. Smith J. Automotive journalist, former editor of Car Craft and Hot Rod. Personal communication: Telephone interview. May 12, 2011.
13. Pitt J. Heat Machine Nationals. *Car Craft.* October 1988:16-27.
14. Danh P. Too Bad T-Bird. *Hot Rod,* November 1986:98-101.
15. Martinez P. Hay, Hay, Take it Away. *Popular Hot Rodding.* July 1989:100-101; 196.
16. Pesterre P. 10 Best. *Popular Hot Rodding.* July 1989:92-93; 84; 100.
17. Baskerville G. Hot Rod Magazine's Top Ten. December 1988:50-53.
18. Hatano B. Kings of Pro Street. *Car Craft.* November 1988:18-28.

# chapter 7
## ROCK ON
## ROCKY ROBERTSON

Ceasar Maragni photo

## chapter 7 | ROCK ON

### *(Dirt) Tracking Down His Automotive Roots*

The screeching high-pitched whine of meshing gears danced among the thunderous cyclical note of open headers. The dampened track surface—unevenly illuminated by the hot glare of soaring lights—shed its most superficial layers of earth with each passing lap. A quick glance from the infield pit revealed the faint silhouettes of a handful of young fans frenzied with activity in the dark and distant corners. But who were they? And what in the world were they doing?

The short answer was that they were the Robertson kids attending a local dirt track race, being caked with the flying mud from the track while they were having the time of their lives.

Such was life for a young Rocky Robertson. By the age of five, he and his younger brother and sister were regulars at the dirt track races near his hometown of Centralia, Illinois. In a simpler time, Rocky recalls roaming the pits, wrenching on cars, and just generally having a good bit of unsupervised adolescent fun. Not much has changed after all these years.

His love for cars was deep and almost immediate. "As a kid, if I wasn't pushing Matchboxes around the piano, I was drawing cars on paper," he said.[1] Long before the pre-teen surge of testosterone would eventually turn his eye in the direction of pretty girls, the young Illinoisan was entranced and infatuated by anything on wheels.

As driving age approached, Robertson's love for going fast moved from dirt to asphalt. "Around 15 or 16, I kind of got out of that [dirt track racing] and really got into drag racing," he admitted. Eighth-mile strips in nearby Benton and Harrisburg were frequent weekend destinations. An occasional street race wasn't out of the question either.

"It was nothing to be out on a country road with 200 people watching street racing. There would be scanners and lookouts," he said. In eighth grade, Robertson got left behind as participants and spectators alike scattered from one such gathering. "Here come the cops from every direction and everybody just took off. I didn't have enough sense to jump in one of their cars, so I ended up going to jail that night," he added with a laugh.

As much fun as racing was, early signs of Robertson's automotive paint and body artistry began to show in high school. "I liked to go fast, but I always wanted my cars to look good, too," he said. In addition to working on his own stuff, he started doing jobs for hire, too. By his sophomore year, he was operating a paint and body shop out of his parents' garage, earning several thousand dollars over the summer doing work mostly for friends.

"Local car shows and stock car races were all forgotten in 1978 when I rolled into Tulsa, Oklahoma, for the National Street Rod Association Street Rod Nationals," he said. "I couldn't believe it. I was transformed—I was hooked with no detox in mind," he said. Always a fan of Novas, Robertson fell in love with several at the event, including a tubbed '64 with a snorkel scoop that reminded him of his very own '64 back home.

By June of 1986, Robertson had built a '69 Nova that landed on the cover of *Popular Hot Rodding*.[2] Complete with full custom 2 x 3 dual rail chassis and a tunnel-rammed big block, it was a runner. With a shimmering brandywine lacquer paintjob with tasteful graphics, it was a looker, too. Robertson had acquired the car in 1980 at the age of 21. He steadily built it up into a potent nine-second street machine, learning chassis work under the tutelage of experienced fabricator Larry Lamczyk.

"It was nothing for me to be down there welding until 3 or 4 in the morning every night," he said. Under Lamsczyk's watchful eye, Robertson honed the skills he would later use to build a number of groundbreaking hot rods all by himself. He had handled all the paint and bodywork alone out of his facility, Performance Body Shop.

Robertson recalled one particular story in the Nova from the Springfield event in 1984. "We pulled into a shopping center and everyone's yelling 'Burn 'em up! Burn 'em up!' and all of the sudden it got really quiet," he said slyly. "To this day I remember somebody yelling 'You ain't got a hair on your a$$ if you don't light 'em up!' I was like, 'F—k. THAT!'—I set the line lock and brought her up to around 5500 rpm and I let her eat. I launched it across the intersection and when I stopped it was like a SWAT team. There were like 20 cops on me!" he said laughing.

As Robertson is fond of saying, the best part of the Nationals for him was always being right in the middle of the action.

## Hot Rodding Goes High Tech

While getting a car on the cover of *PHR* was a dream come true for the young body man and custom car builder, it was a visit to the 1985 Street Machine Nationals in nearby East St. Louis that had Robertson poised to take hot rodding into uncharted waters come time for the 1986 show. A longtime fan of classic Novas, Robertson was blown away by Matt & Debbie Hay's Oldsmobile Ciera. The front-wheel drive late model platform had made for an incredible pro street car. With that concept in mind, he decided to find a similar starting point that he could claim for himself. By the time the feature on the Nova ran in *PHR*, Robertson had already announced his plans to sell the car to finance the build of a new tubbed late model.

"The car that inspired me to turn away from Novas was undoubtedly Matt Hay's Ciera," he said. "Right after the show I started looking around for something kind of like it that had been wrecked that I could rebuild. I was hoping to find a Buick Somerset because they were brand new at the time and I especially loved the full-width taillights in those cars," he added.

Like many street machiners, Robertson had already made hotel reservations in Ionia, Michigan, for the show shortly after it was announced as the site for 1986. Probably more than any other builder, he was thrilled

when he learned the show would instead be moving to Du Quoin, a facility he had frequented to watch Harleys and dirt track races on the "Miracle Mile" track in the '70s. Even though the show was suddenly in his backyard, there was still this small matter of building a brand new pro street car.

Despite calling junkyards and checking every local classifieds paper for a few months, Robertson was still coming up empty handed in his quest for a Somerset. Hope was fading that he would be able to locate a suitable candidate at a reasonable cost. To make matters worse, the clock was ticking and the window of opportunity to complete the complex build in time for the '86 Nationals was closing, too. Robertson had nearly talked himself into settling for a wrecked 1985 Pontiac Grand Am that he had already located during the search.

On the recommendation of employee Jim Schwartz, Robertson contacted a salvage yard in Effingham, just a short trip north of the body shop. A phone call confirmed it—there was a wrecked, low mileage (and apparently hard to find) Buick Somerset with a crunched front clip sitting in the yard. Robertson immediately hooked up his trailer and got on the road. Within a couple of hours, $1,300 had exchanged hands and the Buick was headed from junkyard dog to boulevard bruiser.

Robertson's initial plans for the Somerset included a full tube chassis and a big block Chevy. However, through a convoluted chain of contacts eerily reminiscent of the Kevin Bacon game, Robertson had gained an "in" with Buick in Detroit. In other words, he knew a guy that knew a guy who was a guy who could help him on the path to pro street stardom.

Specifically, chassis mentor Larry Lamczyk had done some work for Southern Illinois pro drag racer Buddy Ingersoll. Ingersoll had been making waves in both the NHRA and IHRA Pro Stock divisions with a wicked-quick turbo V-6 powered pro stocker.[3] The high-tech hot rod was the baby of Buick Special Products Engineering and Director Ron Yuille. Through Ingersoll, Robertson got Yuille's number.

At the time, Buick had significantly increased its motorsports presence, inking marketing deals with NHRA drivers such as Kenny Bernstein and NASCAR great Bobby Allison. Robertson's timing was perfect, as the

Somerset project fit well within the overall push to establish Buick as a performance brand. At the same time, the company's emerging "outlaw" reputation was a dead on match for Robertson's persona, too. It was a natural fit. His call to Yuille was well received and when Buick asked Robertson to submit a formal proposal, he gladly obliged.

Within a few weeks, Yuille had successfully pushed the request for assistance through and Buick's marketing package was really starting to come together. After hearing Robertson further detail his vision for the car, conversation turned to plans for propulsion. "I told him I was planning to put a big block Chevy in it, mostly because of the cost savings over anything else" he recounted. "Ron said, 'No, no—we'd like you to put a turbo Grand National motor in it. Do you have a problem with that?' I told him no and he said, 'We'll send you one.' Three or four days later, I get a brand new V-6 GN Turbo motor in a crate to my door," he said.[4]

The most challenging part of the build was yet to come. "I get everything built and fabricated and got the car all ready. But it is May and I still don't have the thing wired up," he recalled. "Buick pulled an electrical engineer that was at Indy for the 500 and sent him in a rental car to my shop," he added. With a 30-foot long schematic push-pinned to the shop wall, Robertson and the brainiac from Buick worked for two weeks to wire the car and get the intercooled Grand National turbo motor running.[1] It would be the first-ever pro street car with electronic fuel injection.[5]

Robertson finished the Somerset in time for Du Quoin in 1986, and it was an instant success. In addition to taking the cover of the November '86 *Hot Rod,* it also earned a full color spread in the March '87 *Car Craft* and June '87 *PHR*, as well.[5-7] At least a decade before pro touring would become all the rage, Robertson had managed to construct a 10-second street car that wouldn't overheat while cruising the fairgrounds and would routinely get 20 mpg or better on the highway. The car walked away with a very respectable third place finish in the CE Pro Street award behind Matt Hay and Rick Dobbertin.[8]

Robertson took the car back to the Nats in '87 after further refining a few aspects of the build, again taking third place in the CE Pro Street cat-

egory.[9] However, he started to get annoyed by the fact that the car simply wasn't drawing the attention he thought it should.

"It had a flat hood. People would actually come up to me and ask, 'Where's the blower?' They just didn't get it," he said sharply. The car was no slouch in its own right, garnering a Hot Rod Top Ten for '86 and was widely praised by the magazines and aftermarket who saw the future in the build.

However, in an era of screaming wild paint jobs, multi-stage superchargers, and exotic induction systems, the relatively mild GM garnet red metallic, single turbo V-6 was, in Robertson's estimation, a bit too subtle and understated to be fully appreciated at the time. The Centralia native was ready for the next step in his pro street progression, and again his friends at Buick were ready to pitch in.

### *Pretty (Awesome) In Pink*

"They were releasing a new LeSabre T-Type as a spin-off of the Grand National," Robertson said. After talking with Buick corporate and deciding to build one, Robertson said Buick had a new shell delivered and ready for fabrication. Wowed by the stainless steel chassis of Dobbertin's J-2000, Robertson decided to go with a stainless chassis of his own for the new car. He also admitted that as enjoyable as the Somerset had been to build and drive, his goals for the LeSabre were different altogether.

"I wanted to play the game. I wanted to build a fairground car," he said.

With a cool new late model body on the rack and a stainless chassis in the works, there were still some details to work out. Determined to make a splash with color this time around, Robertson opted for a custom mixed 'Miami Vice' pink. Motorvation for the car would again be in the form of a high tech Buick V-6, this time outfitted with a highly detailed Kinsler injection system.

Unfortunately, the demanding build dragged on until the eleventh hour leading up to the 1988 Street Machine Nationals. Robertson was actually in the paint booth on Friday the weekend of the show. To make matters worse, he suffered a terrible setback during the job that would ultimately cost him a chance at any professionally judged awards that year.

"It was 9 a.m. on Friday—the day the show had started. We had wet sanded the car and I went through the paint in a bunch of places. I pulled it out in the sun to take a look before we shot the clear on it and I was like 'Oh s---! We've gotta repaint the f---ing car!'" he said dejectedly.

"The show had already started. I hadn't slept in like three or four days. It was like 90 degrees. I had five or six guys helping me color sand and I literally had towels duct taped to my paint arm to keep from dripping sweat in the paint when I'm re-spraying color coat," he recalled.

With the clear coat still soft, Robertson loaded the car up and headed to the Fairgrounds. Unfortunately, the throng of traffic was too deep and Robertson missed the noon entry cut-off by about 30 minutes. Although the car was undoubtedly one of the trickest pieces of machinery on the grounds, it would only be eligible for participant-voted awards.

Despite the obvious disappointment of building a car from scratch over the course of an entire year and taking just 30 minutes too long to do so, the car was very well received. Robertson's son Conner made the October '88 *Car Craft* as he helped polish up the ride at the show. It would go on to be featured in all three major magazines, and was named to *Popular Hot Rodding*'s "10 Best Pro Street Cars Ever Built" list in 1989.[10-12]

Although not eligible for the prestigious Best Pro Street award, the car did receive a number of participant and fan vote awards, including Best General Motors and runner-up Best Overall Street Machine.[13] It would also later go on to win the Best Pro Street and Best Overall Street Machine at the 1988 Street Machine Nationals East as well as Best Pro Street award at the 1989 Hot Rod Supernationals, too.[12,14,15] The car fared well at Du Quoin in 1989, but the fact that it was a year old car didn't help come judging time. Robertson took second in Pro Street and first in Best GM.[16]

Robertson insists that the one-upmanship of the era was fierce, but it certainly was the impetus to build wilder and crazier cars. "As much as you hated seeing cars like Rick's and Matt's come to an event you attended, it pushed you," he said. "I think knowing that cars of that caliber would be

there drove all of us, and ultimately it was great for the magazines and the fans," he added.

Unfortunately, the near miss of judging at the '88 show would strike again when a deal to have the car made into a model kit in the same series as Dobbertin's J-2000 and Hay's T-Bird fell through with Revell.[17] With the deal all but done, the *Hot Rod* model series was scrapped before the LeSabre was able to enter production.

By 1990, Robertson still owned the car but wasn't planning to take it to the Nationals since it was now going on three years old. "My buddies were telling me I had to take it. My philosophy is simple: If I'm not the show, I don't want to go," he said.

However, an ultra-cool salt spray graphics job on a GMC Bonneville racer got Robertson thinking it was time to freshen the LeSabre. The intricate design—now relatively straightforward to mask using a computer and digital plotter—would have to be drawn by hand on a huge 4 x 8 sheet and hand cut from frisket film on the car.

Although tedious, the effort was good enough to land the car another feature in *Popular Hot Rodding* as well as Best Pro Street for the 1990 SM Nats and Best Graphics for the '91 show.[18-20]

## Kickin' It Old School

Robertson's established reputation as a master craftsman was enough to keep him front and center in the pro street spotlight even without building another new car in the early '90s. He was an integral member of the "Mild to Wild in 55 Hours" team at the '91 show, but was still searching for direction on his next build. As the "Dare to Be Different" trend began to take hold, Robertson got the itch to build his next creation using an older body style.

A partial tongue-in-cheek article in *Car Craft* predicted that the man who brought pro street into the electronic age was destined for even more cutting edge, late model stardom.[21] Buick had already offered up their new Reatta as a potential starting point.[1] However, while thumbing through a

*Hemmings Motor News* in 1993, he stumbled across a photo of a Kaiser Special and immediately fell in love.[22]

Liking the car was one thing. Finding one was quite another. Originally produced between 1947 and 1955, the cars were relatively rare. As luck would have it, Robertson spotted the distinctive tail end of a straight '51 hanging out of an old lean-to just 20 miles from his house. For $300 less than he had paid for a wrecked Somerset seven years prior, he bagged his next target, took it home, and got to work.[22]

The end result was a fantastic display of Robertson's growth and versatility as a builder. A gorgeous polished stainless steel frame provided the backbone. The sparkling 2 x 3 inch boxed frame rails were polished to perfection by close friend Kevin Rogers who was instrumental in the build. Meanwhile, a potent GM 502 cubic inch crate motor with twin Paxton superchargers provided the muscle. Throw in the requisite fat Mickey Thompson rear meats and a slick never-goes-out-of-style black with orange flames paint job and you have a well-executed machine.[22]

Sadly, by the time the Kaiser was done, the Nationals had already started their decline. Robertson dutifully attended the show in Du Quoin even though all magazine coverage had dried up and gone elsewhere. At the same time, he also attended a number of other shows, actually debuting it at the 1994 Hot Rod Power Fest in Indy. He also entered the Car Craft Summer Cruise, new for 1994, as well. Touted on the cover of the October 1994 issue as the "Summer's Hottest New Event," in the words of Robertson, "That show *sucked*." At just around 600 cars, it paled in comparison to the Nationals. He had a point.

## *A Pirate's Life*

These days, Robertson is content—and busier than ever—running his modest hot rod shop in Albers, Illinois. The LeSabre sits in his showroom, contentedly resting and reflecting on her storied past. And while he still manages to do his fair share of custom work on autos, it has interestingly

been a handful of vehicles of the floating variety that have managed to take up much of the prolific builder's time these days.

"When I was going to the Street Machines, it was crazy. A lot of the guys I competed with would go to the show and then spend the evenings holed up in their hotel rooms. Not me," he recounted. "I was almost always in the streets, partying and partaking in all the crazy s--- going on," he said. However, once those opportunities stopped, he says he was left feeling empty and without direction.

In addition to the limelight and the partying, Robertson says he missed the family aspect. His sons Robbie, Connor, and Austin were regulars on the show circuit. Former wife Laurie had been instrumental in the builds and was right by his side for much of his rise to prominence, as well. Robertson's mom, Donna, stitched upholstery for many of his cars and his step-dad Duane Dudley, who passed away in September 2011, was also a tremendous help transporting the car and prepping for shows. However, these days, Robertson says it just isn't the same.

"The shows you go to now—especially the street rods—they are nice cars, but they all have the same stuff. It is all store-bought," he said with disdain. He has also noticed that the folks attending the shows have changed over the years—and not for the better. "Dude, there is NOTHING fun about going to a car show and seeing a bunch of 40 or 50-year-old women in halter tops," he added with a hearty chuckle.

To fill the wild void left by the exit of the Nats, Rocky was first introduced to Lake of the Ozarks in 1998. A vibrant social hotspot, the 54,000 acre reservoir is the site for boating, skiing, and riding personal watercraft all summer long. By 1999, Robertson was so smitten by the lifestyle that he purchased his own 30' craft, a Profile power boat. Robertson has tricked out the vessel with custom graphics and added a number of other unique touches.

"What I basically had done to hot rods all my life, I started doing to my boat," he said. With flames, custom-fabbed pieces and parts, and other evidence of his auto-tricking past, the boat was a hit with the lakers. And just like old times, Robertson is always happy to draw a crowd, especially if the crowd members are mostly good looking partiers of the female persuasion scantily clad in bikinis.

Robertson says he has been a regular at the lake—some 200 miles from his home in Albers—ever since '99. "When that whole car show deal ended, I was miserable. This boat became my Street Machine Nationals," he said. Like a retired athlete looking to fill the void, the lake has been a welcome addition to his life. Always content to be at the epicenter of any party, Robertson says that he still has run-ins with the authorities from time to time; however, it is no longer because he's doing burnouts in the parking lot.

It seems he hasn't figured out how to install the line lock on the boat just yet.

## *References*

1. Robertson R. Custom car builder. Personal communication: Telephone interview. May 20, 2013.
2. Benty C. Street Lethal. *Popular Hot Rodding.* June 1986:32-33; 84.
3. Baechtel J. Hot Air Regal. *Hot Rod.* April 1986:69-74; 146.
4. Robertson R. Custom car builder. Personal communication: Telephone interview. May 16, 2011.
5. Smith J. Roadmaster. *Car Craft.* March 1987:62-66.
6. Baechtel J. Prom Queen. *Hot Rod.* November 1986:60-65.
7. Pesterre P. Rapid Red Rocket. *Popular Hot Rodding.* June 1987:66-67.
8. Anand D. Street Machine Nationals. *Car Craft.* October 1986:23-32.
9. Bernsau T. Street Machine Nationals. *Car Craft.* October 1987:32-45.
10. Pesterre P. 10 Best. *Popular Hot Rodding.* July 1989:92-93; 84; 100.
11. Smith J. LeSabre Rattling. *Hot Rod,* November 1988:70-73.
12. Pitt J. Look Sharp. *Car Craft.* April 1990:98-99.
13. Pitt J. Heat Machine Nationals. *Car Craft.* October 1988:16-27.
14. Anderson S. Super Nationals '89. *Hot Rod.* September 1989:22-31.
15. Benty C. The Street Machine Nationals East. *Car Craft.* January 1989:102-105.
16. Pitt J. The Best Ever! Street Machine Nationals. *Car Craft.* October 1989:21-32.
17. Sexton E. Project Manager, Revell, Inc. Personal communication: Telephone interview. June 10, 2011.
18. Rathbun C. Street Machine Nats '90. *Car Craft.* October 1990:18-43.
19. Bernsau T. Street Machine Nationals. *Car Craft.* October 1990:18-31.

20. Fetherston D. Run 'N Low. *Popular Hot Rodding.* November 1990:100-101.
21. Pitt J. Future Street. *Car Craft.* May 1990:36-40.
22. Baskerville G. Rocky's Roller. *Hot Rod.* December 1994:92-93.

# chapter 8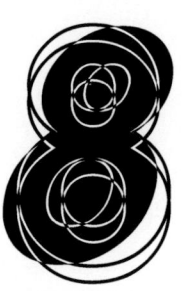

## PARADISE CITY "WOODSTOCK ON WHEELS" ROLLS INTO DU QUOIN 1986-1989

Ceasar Maragni photo

## chapter 8 | PARADISE CITY

*Take me down to the paradise city*
*Where the grass is green and the girls are pretty*
*Take me home [x2]*
*Oh would you please take me home*
*I wanna go*
*Oh would you please take me home*
*Take me down to the paradise city*
*Where the grass is green and the girls are pretty*
*Take me home [x3]*

"Paradise City," by Axl Rose, Saul Hudson, Duff McKagan, Izzy Stradlin, Steven Adler; © copyright 1987, Universal Music Publishing Corp.[1]

## Under New Management

After the 1985 Street Machine Nationals in East St. Louis—universally described as the most miserable Nats in history—the show was once again looking for a home. At the same time, the show and other such Petersen events had been sold to Indianapolis-based Special Events. Founder and CEO Bruce Hubley took the reins and promptly went to work to secure a suitable location for 1986.

Hubley was no stranger to the Nationals. He and his company had first been tapped to help during the second year of the show in 1978 and had remained involved ever since. Special Events had initially been brought aboard by show founder Harry Hibler and *Car Craft* Publisher Steve Green to help sell tickets to the public. With considerable help from Hubley and his charges, spectator count nearly tripled the first year Special Events was aboard.[2,3] At the same time, the Petersen folks continued their efforts to bring cars to the event.

Almost immediately after the disastrous '85 event, the search was on for a new spot. Eventually, a tentative agreement was struck to host the show at the Ionia Free Fair in Ionia, Michigan.[4,5] Located between Grand Rapids and Lansing, Ionia had a population of just 2,842 at the time of the 1980 census.[6] Participants had concerns that the venue was too small and that lodging would be sparse.[7,8] Despite those shortcomings, the Free Fair's 40+ acres of mowed, shaded, and landscaped land would be a refreshing change from the East St. Louis facility's endless acres of asphalt and unobstructed sun.[9] Or would it?

Shortly after the site selection had been announced, city fathers had a change of heart and backed out of the deal. Hubley was back to square one with the 1986 show rapidly approaching. "At that point in time, we had to hustle to put together a deal with another venue," he said.[5]

Enter Du Quoin.

## Center of the Universe

As luck would have it, the picturesque Du Quoin State Fairgrounds (DSF) had recently been acquired by the state of Illinois and the new management was hungry to attract events in order to make the underperforming operation profitable again. With Governor James R. Thompson's blessing, the wildest show on wheels was moving again. This time, however, it was headed for a facility in the middle of a cornfield on the outskirts of a town no one had ever heard of.

The gorgeous 1,500+ acre venue had been founded by local Bill Hayes and his family in 1923 and eventually sold to Iraqi investor Saad Jaber in 1979.[10] Jaber hit hard times financially, ultimately borrowing several hundred thousand dollars from the state just to host the fair in 1985.[11] The state loaned the money to the troubled financier on the condition that Jaber would sell the facility to the state the following year.

In early 1986, the fairgrounds changed hands as promised. When the state took possession, their top priority was to bring in a major national event.[12,13] Coupled with Special Events' pressing need for a place to host the Nats, it was a match made in heaven.

"Harry [Hibler], Bruce [Hubley], and I went down to Du Quoin to take a look at it and it was like going from the worst possible venue [in East St. Louis] to the best possible venue," recalled then-*Car Craft* Editor Jeff Smith.[14] "Du Quoin was so big, it would allow us—for the first time—to have room for *all* the cars. Lots of hills, green grass, the lake with the wildlife—it was great. It was just fantastic," he added.

Hibler, Hubley, and Smith were convinced that they had at long last found the home the Nats had so desperately needed. However, the downside was the geography. Compared to previous sites, Du Quoin was extremely isolated. With the nearest major city, St. Louis, over an hour and a half away and hotel rooms in the immediate vicinity of the DSF complex numbering only in the hundreds, organizers had grave concerns that despite the grounds' grandeur and size, the town simply would not be able to accommodate a massive influx of 5,000 cars and more than 100,000 people.

However, the perceived limitation actually served to be a blessing in disguise. With none of the small towns in the area able to provide enough hotel rooms for the entire throng, showgoers and participants were forced to disburse. Some stayed in Carbondale. Others stayed in Benton. Procrastinators who failed to get reservations until the last minute were exiled to further reaches such as Mt. Vernon some 50 miles away and even Paducah, Kentucky over two hours away. At least early on, the spreading of the Nats crowd helped to ease the burden the show had placed on Indy and Springfield.

So scarce were hotels in the area that Special Events staffers working the event were not even given the option of staying in traditional rooms. Instead, the Governor's Mansion on the DSF grounds was used. Far from lavish, the home that appeared palatial from the outside was nearly completely empty inside. The state hadn't yet had a chance to furnish the newly acquired property. Sleeping bags in hand, show personnel roughed it on the floor for the entire weekend.[15]

Following the announcement of the show, word began travelling fast around town about the horde of high performance street machines and the cloud of 100,000 rowdy fans that had already been kicked out of three towns in five years. Special Events tried to quell those mounting fears in May. Event Director Chuck Ross was confident, saying the show would be "...no major problem for the Illinois State Police."[16]

In addition to Illinois State Police, event organizers had also tapped into nearby Southern Illinois University Carbondale for some extra muscle. Football players were hired to help bolster security for the weekend and many could be seen all across the grounds. Sporting overly tight yellow t-shirts and an occasional walkie-talkie, their primary job was to break up fights and prevent burnouts. One such player who worked the event was Saluki offensive lineman J.P. Watters.

"One of my teammates knew a guy who knew a guy who was helping set up the show and they needed security. Me and about 20 or so other guys were in town for the summer and we couldn't say yes fast enough. It sounded like fun," Watters said.[17]

The team members operated as a manpower aid for the Illinois State Police, who had assigned a total of 300 officers to work crowd and traffic control at the event at some point during the weekend.[18] It was, at the time, the biggest operation in the history of the Illinois State Police.[18]

Saturday night proved to be somewhat taxing for the force. Otherwise, officers, townspeople, and promoters alike were thrilled that the show had come and gone with no serious injuries and relatively few problems.[18] In fact, some showgoers complained that the whole event had been "too conservative," claiming they probably wouldn't return in '87 if it came back to Du Quoin.[19]

Politicians and spectators aside, the cars that showed up in '86 were impressive and helped kick off the first-ever Du Quoin event in style. Iconic cars still discussed in pro street circles to this day were in attendance. The Hays' Ciera took the Pro Street title but faced fierce competition from the likes of Rod Saboury's '63 Corvette, Rocky Robertson's '86 Buick Somerset, Mark Grimes' '65 Malibu, and of course, Rick Dobbertin's Pontiac J-2000. Pro street was alive and well.

Interestingly, naysayers of the pro street movement had been predicting its demise almost since its infancy in the late '70s and early '80s. The fat tire and wild powerplant look was beginning to hit its stride in '86, and nowhere was that fact more apparent than at the Du Quoin State Fairgrounds. By the time the show hit Southern Illinois, roughly one out of every two features in *Car Craft* involved a tubbed street machine.

Despite the incredible cars, fan turnout for the show had been slightly lower than expected (62,124).[20] On the other hand, total car count, limited to just 3,000 for the first year at the venue, had been easily met.[20] Governor Thompson, who had flown down from Springfield by helicopter just to witness the event firsthand, was thoroughly impressed. The estimated $4 million dollar injection into the Southern Illinois economy wasn't bad, either.[21] Before the weekend's end, event organizers had already been invited back. '87 was a done deal.[19,20]

## Ya'll Come Back Now

Encouraged by a smooth operation in 1986, hopes were high for a repeat performance in '87. As *Car Craft* staffer Tim Bernsau would write, "After a few years of bouncing from city to city like high horsepower refugees, people were glad to be in a town that seemed to genuinely welcome them."[22] That sentiment would change dramatically with the passage of time.

The 1987 show featured a Street Machine Nationals first: rain on two of the three days of the event.[23] However, not even a couple of thunderstorms were enough to dampen the spirits of the crowd of 65,000 onlookers. The place was jumping.

*Car Craft* again gushed over the awesomeness of their newfound home. "The Du Quoin State Fairgrounds has got to be *the* perfect spot for the Nats," wrote staffer Tim Bernsau.[23] Added attractions such waterskiing exhibitions and radio controlled boat races only added to the excitement, as did another recent development: the three-man balloon launcher.

Called the "Winger," the contraption was simple enough. A huge piece of elastic tubing was held at the ends by two friends and drawn back and released by another. Its sole purpose was to launch water balloons hundreds of feet in the air in the general vicinity of friends, perfect strangers, or even an unsuspecting water skier or two from time to time. Nats veteran and Ridetech Founder Bret Voelkel recalled a tale involving the gadget.

"We got into one incident in the Holiday Inn in Marion," Voelkel said.[24] "Some buddies and I got this new-fangled three-man slingshot that threw water balloons. We decided it was the coolest thing we had ever seen—that we could actually launch a water balloon all the way over the top of the hotel," he added, snickering. Just for fun, Voelkel and his friends proceeded to do just that and—unbeknownst to them—struck the windshield of a parked Illinois State Police cruiser idling in the lot behind the building.

"So this water balloon immediately takes out the windshield—so here come the cops and, being the great friends that we were, we immediately pointed directly at the one of us who just happened to be pulling back on the launcher at the time," he said with a hearty laugh.

It probably wasn't too funny in the moment, as the implicated friend was hauled off in handcuffs. He emerged from jail only after Voelkel and the rest of the gang bailed him out.[24]

## Keep On Rollin'

*Car Craft* seemed convinced that the problems of the past Nats were forever in the rear-view, with a relatively trouble-free 11th annual show in '87 to prove it. "Each year, some of the problems that come with large crowds come back. Until 1987," wrote *CC's* Bernsau.[23] Even sister publication *Hot Rod* was getting in on the love fest, likening Du Quoin to the "...perfect gathering of high performance street machines...in a picturesque setting of wide open cruse lanes, rolling hills, and shade trees."[25] For a time, everything seemed perfect.

Local media outlets seemed satisfied, too. The *Southern Illinoisan* pointed out that the crowd—some 3,000 stronger in number in '87 than in '86—was remarkably well behaved.[26] Although there were dozens of arrests for drunk driving, disorderly conduct, and various moving violations, the show had again mostly sidestepped any major violent crimes. Maybe the Nats and her attendees were finally growing up, after all.

As far as cars went, '87 was a whole lot of the same. Familiar rides from Dobbertin, Hay, Grimes, and Robertson all competed again, this time with Dobbertin capturing the Pro Street title. Only a handful of new builds were revealed, with Wayne Bushey's radical red '64 Nova wagon and Charlie Teidt's late model pro street Vette vying for some of the spotlight. An unknown teenager from up the interstate in Manteno also made the trip in his Porsche red mild pro street '66 Chevelle. That same teenager—Troy Trepanier of modern-day Rad Rides by Troy fame—would return in '88 with the car painted pink.

What spectators couldn't have known about an '87 show with so few new cars revealed was that most of the major players in pro street already had their eye on 1988. Hay, Grimes, Robertson, and Scott Sullivan had each either started or were planning major builds for the next year. It was shaping up to be the best ever.

### And So It Was

I'll come right out and say it: there has never been a more impressive gathering of freshly built, cutting edge, high-end pro street cars than the 1988 Street Machine Nationals. Oh sure, there were several noteworthy cars that made a splash prior to 1988, and there have been plenty of awesome cars in the years since. But the sheer volume of breathtaking, one-of-a-kind street machines that showgoers witnessed in 1988 may never be duplicated. It was unbelievable.

Nearly everyone who was anyone in the pro street game rolled out a trick new build just in time for the event. It was like Sonny Liston, Joe Frasier, Muhammed Ali, George Foreman, and Mike Tyson had all climbed into the ring at the same time—each one throwing the deadliest haymaker they could muster—in hopes of annihilating his opponents. Two blowers from Hay were countered by three blowers from Grimes. Monochrome pink from Robertson was countered by monochrome Cheez Whiz from Sullivan. The build quality just kept getting better, and the competition was fierce. High style was in style.

The only thing hotter than the cars was the weather. Temperatures soared above 100 degrees, topping out at 103 on Saturday. Humidity percolated at a stifling 70%. Heat illnesses and dehydration were common.

Jeff Smith, who had switched over into the Editor's chair at *Hot Rod* recalled the sensation of his shoes sinking into the molten tar-and-chip roads, nearly losing them in the soft black goo on more than one occasion.[14] The cruise routes had been near-liquefied in the searing summer sun. Tires and tarmac endlessly crackled and popped with complaint as the endless stream of hot cars rolled through, nearly glued to the road surface in the process. As *CC* staffer Jerry Pitt would put it, "While Mother Nature tried her best to dominate with the hottest weather she could muster, the gods of performance smiled above."[27]

## chapter 8 | PARADISE CITY

### *Two's Company, a Hundred Thousand's a Crowd*

One hundred and one THOUSAND. Think about that number for a second. From June 23-25, 1989, Du Quoin's population of around 6,000 residents multiplied 17-fold.[28] For one weekend in June, the Du Quoin State Fairgrounds had almost as many residents as Peoria.

Trepanier—the kid from up the road in Manteno—was back. This time his Chevelle sported silky smooth Steve Stanford inspired graphics and a trick set of one-off brushed Boyd's billets. Danny Taylor of Taylor's House of Colors in Louisville, Kentucky, brought out a slick '80s Malibu. Neil Jacobs' blown and injected Hemi '64 Belvidere missed out on pro street judging because it was too old for the '67 cutoff, a problem shared by Sullivan's '55 the year before. Rod Saboury was back with another trick Vette. If the Nats were a wine, the '89 vintage would go down in history as a very *very* good year.

Late-model pro streeters continued to trend upward. The Hays' Thunderbird was back, as was Grimes' Eurosport and Robertson's LeSabre. Rich Gebhardt rolled out a trick new citrus-colored Beretta, while Tom Davis's Sullivan-painted black and aqua version of the new Chevy bodystyle also impressed. Fueled by the popularity of NHRA pro stock versions of the little Bowtie front wheel drive, they were the first of many more to come.

Attendance figures for the weekend went through the roof. Armed with an expanded marketing budget and a steadily growing rep as the greatest car show on Earth, Family Events got spectators to flock to Du Quoin like never before. It would mark the first of nine straight years of more than 100,000 bodies on the grounds. After some tumultuous early years, the Nationals had settled in and seemed to finally be hitting stride.

The grass *was* green. The girls *were* pretty. The Nats had at last found their home.

And to quote Axl Rose, "Yeahhhhheayeah."

## *References*

1. Wikipedia. Paradise City. 2013; http://en.wikipedia.org/wiki/Paradise_City. Accessed March 12, 2013.
2. Caldwell B. Street Machines March on Indianapolis! *Car Craft*. October 1977:46-53.
3. Vogelin R. '78 Street Machine Nationals. *Car Craft*. October 1978:26-34; 106.
4. Smith J. National Report. *Car Craft*. March 1986:101-102.
5. Hubley B. Founder and CEO of Family Events, Inc. Personal communication: Telephone interview. May 22, 2012.
6. U.S. Department of Commerce. 1980 Census of Population and Housing. 1982; ftp://www.nwmcog.org/HistoricDecennialCensus/Census-1980-Michigan.pdf. Accessed March 7, 2013.
7. Robertson R. Custom car builder. Personal communication: Telephone interview. May 16, 2011.
8. Carter J. I miss the good 'ole STREET MACHINE NATIONALS! 2009; http://www.yellowbullet.com/forum/showthread.php?t=193327. Accessed June 29, 2011.
9. Ionia Free Fair. 2012; http://pama.org/ioniaff/about/about-us.php. Accessed May 12, 2013.
10. Mathes C. Du Quoin's Fred Huff Compiles History of Favored Event. *The Southern Illinoisan*. August 14, 2002.
11. Huff F. Lifelong Du Quoin resident and former Manager of the Du Quoin State Fair. Personal communication: Telephone interview. May 19, 2011.
12. Mason J. Executive I, Illinois Department of Agriculture, Du Quoin State Fair. Personal communication: Telephone interview. May 20, 2011
13. Hill N. Du Quoin State Fair. Personal communication: Telephone interview. May 20, 2011

14. Smith J. Automotive journalist, former editor of Car Craft and Hot Rod. Personal communication: Telephone interview. May 12. 2011.
15. Davis S. Former Director of Events, Special Events, Inc. Personal communication: Telephone interview. June 29. 2012.
16. Sickler L. 'Knock on wood'. *The Southern Illinoisan*. May 16, 1986.
17. Watters JP. Former football player and Street Machine Nationals security. Personal communication. May 15, 2012.
18. Landis T. 'Worst' Didn't Happen. *The Southern Illinoisan*. June 30, 1986.
19. Weil N. They'll Be Back. *The Southern Illinoisan*. June 30, 1986: 1.
20. Landis T. Car Show Shines in Thompson's Eye. *The Southern Illinoisan*. June 29, 1986.
21. Davidson J. Street Machine Nationals Attendance Put at 62,124. *Du Quoin Evening Call*. June 30, 1986: 8.
22. Bernsau T. *The Best of the Street Machine Nationals, 1972-1993*. Los Angeles, CA: Petersen Publishing Company; 1993.
23. Bernsau T. Street Machine Nationals. *Car Craft*. October 1987:32-45.
24. Voelkel B. Ridetech Founder. Personal communication: Telephone interview. April 17, 2012.
25. Smith J. Supercar Summer Fun. *Hot Rod*. November 1987:22.
26. Weil N, Landis T. Let the Good Times Roll! *The Southern Illinoisan*. June 28, 1987.
27. Pitt J. Heat Machine Nationals. *Car Craft*. October 1988:16-27.
28. Pitt J. The Best Ever! Street Machine Nationals. *Car Craft*. October 1989:21-32.

# Nats in Pics

**First Time in Du Quoin**
*These images were snapped by Ceasar Maragni at the 1986 Street Machine Nationals at the Du Quoin State Fairgrounds. That's Matt & Debbie Hay's Oldsmobile in the top left.*

**Grounds Pounding**
*With acres of rolling hills and miles of cruising, the Du Quoin State Fairgrounds provided the perfect venue for the Nats. Usually in excess of 200 Illinois State Troopers worked the event.* Ceasar Maragni photos

**Just Enjoyin' the Show**
*Street Machine Nationals, Du Quoin State Fairgrounds, 1986.*
Ceasar Maragni photos

125

### A Lil' Somethin' for Everybody
*The '86 Nationals featured 3000 cars, including Rod Saboury's huffed and tubbed 1963 Corvette (right).*
Ceasar Maragni photos

**Let the Good Times Roll**
*After a scorching hot and traffic-plagued '85 show in East St. Louis, the 10th Annual installment of the even in Du Quoin in 1986 was a hit with both with participants and spectators alike.*
　　　　　　*Ceasar Maragni photos*

**Just Wow.**
It is still unclear if Rick Dobbertin's license plate ("BLOWN") was in reference to the J-2000's incredible induction system or the car's typical effect on the minds of those who checked it out. The car debuted in '86 and was a crowd favorite at Du Quoin.
*Ceasar Maragni photos*

Scott Sullivan photo

### The One That Started It All
*Scott Sullivan's 1967 Nova*

James Brooks photo

James Brooks photo

**Bi-PRO-lar**
*No two cars in the pro street era were more recognizable—or more fundamentally different—than Sullivan's '55 Chevy and Dobbertin's J-2000.*

133

**In-NOVA-tor**
*Dobbertin's '64 Nova.*
Photos provided

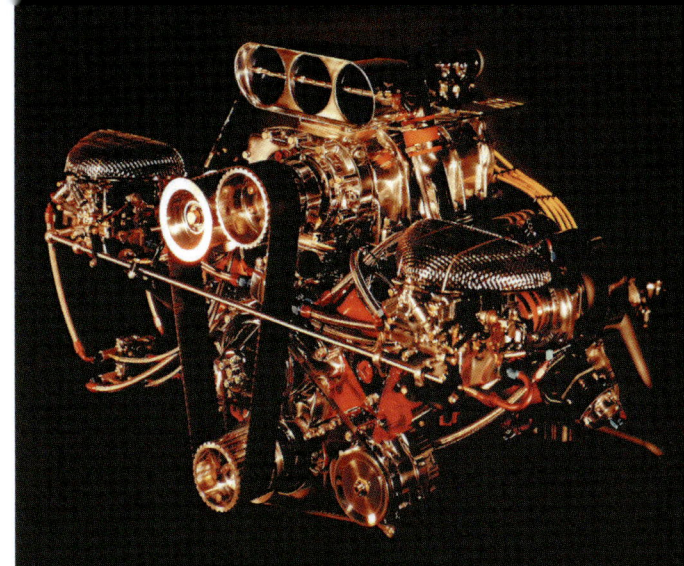

135

### Are We There Yet?
*Dobbertin's J-2000 once hit 500 miles per hour. Granted, it was in the belly of a jumbo jet headed for Australia, but still...*
Photos provided

**Hay Wagons**
*Matt & Debbie Hay were regulars at the Street Machine Nationals. Over the years, their cars got more and more wild. Their pink Thunderbird was made into a Revell model kit.*

*Marc Telder photos except as indicated*

### Old School Muscle to New School Tech
*A life-long fan of Novas, Rocky Robertson departed from convention in a big way with his fuel injected V-6 Buick Somerset.*

*Photos provided except as indicated*

Marc Telder photo

**All New Low**
Robertson's iconic Buick LeSabre was the epitome of fairgrounds cool. He still owns the car he fabbed from scratch over 20 years ago.
Photos provided except as indicated

James Brooks photo

Marc Telder photo

**Still Rock-in'**
Unless he's on the lake, Robertson stays busy at his shop in Albers, Illinois. Below is the LeSabre and Kaiser at the 1995 Street Machine Nationals.
*Ceasar Maragni photos except as indicated*

Marc Telder photo

Butch Pate photo

### Let's Get Rocked
*Robertson's creations on display at the 1995 Street Machine Nationals (top left); the twin-supercharged 502 and polished stainless chassis of the Kaiser (middle left), 27-foot Sleekcraft boat with custom skull graphics (bottom left); Billy Wooten's Chevelle with Robertson paint & graphics; and Rocky with his grandson Tyler (center)*
All photos provided except as indicated

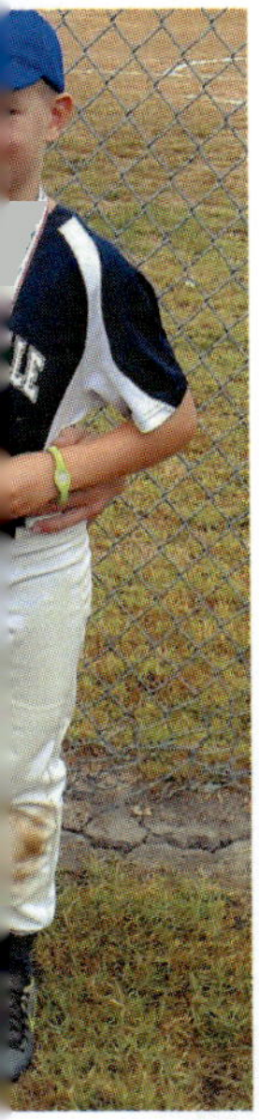

### Geeze, It Is Hot Out Here
*Shirts were in short supply at the '89 Nats in Du Quoin as temps were scorching and humidity was stifling. Rich Gebhardt's smokin' hot Beretta wasn't helping matters either. Onlookers crowded the car all weekend.*

James Brooks photo

145

**Not Your Father's Oldsmobile**
*Jimmy Weishaar's Gebhardt-built 1990 Olds Cutlass at the '91 Street Machine Nationals (above).*
Marc Telder photo

**Get Your Goat**
*Mike Lloyd's Gebhardt-built '70 Pontiac GTO at the '92 Street Machine Nationals (above and right).*
Marc Telder photo (above); Butch Pate photo (right)

**Grimes Time**
*Mark Grimes'
1965 Malibu.
Grimes still owns
the car today.*
   *Marc Telder photos*

### Overblown
*Grimes followed up the Malibu with a triple-blown '87 Chevy Eurosport in 1988.*
James Brooks photos

### LAUNCH
*Troy Trepanier's '66 Chevelle (and wife Angela on the right) at the Nats in 1989.*
James Brooks photo

**Pro Box**
*Troy Trepanier's '60 Impala was the star of the 1990 Nats.*
Annette Zimbelman photo except as indicated

Marc Telder photo

Marc Telder photo

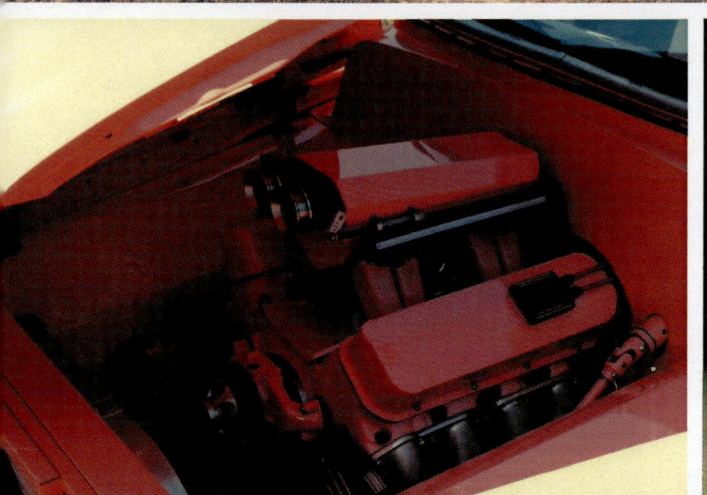

### Bumongous
*Trepanier followed up Pro Box with this trick 1950 Buick Roadmaster, seen here at the 1992 Nats in Du Quoin.*
*James Brooks photo*

### Rumblur
*This 1960 Dodge Rambler was the last car Trepanier ever built for himself. Although no magazines were present, Trepanier still showed the build off in Du Quoin at the 1994 Street Machine Nationals.*

*Annette Zimbelman photo provided*

Marc Telder photo

James Brooks photo

**Oh, Canada**
*Al Hinds debuted his multi-hued Beretta (top) in 1990 and followed it up with his teal Lumina (bottom) in 1992.*

**PSSSSST**
*Bret Voelkel's air ride equipped '70 Mustang debuted in 1996.*

*Bret Voelkel photo provided*

**Imitation is the Sincerest Form of Stealing**
*Bret Voelkel's '70 Mustang (left) was featured in the October 1986* Car Craft *and was a regular at the Nats. My first car, a '72 Nova (below) was neither. But my dad and I did shamelessly pilfer the Taylor's House of Colors paint scheme using this Polaroid as a guide.*

*Toby Brooks photos*

153

**Hoosier Daddy**
*Voelkel's air ride equipped '70 Mustang was featured on the cover of* Popular Hot Rodding's *first-ever issue featuring Street Machine Nationals coverage in October 1996.*
Bret Voelkel photos provided

154

Marc Telder photo

Marc Telder photo

### Lining the Streets
Crowds at the Nats always flocked to see the nasty pro street machinery coming. All of these cruising images were snapped in 1986.

Marc Telder photo

**Still Kickin'**
The 1998 edition of the show still featured plenty of cool cars and smiling faces, but undoubtedly fewer than past years.

Butch Pate photos

157

### Rub-A-Tub-Tub
*Despite a lack of pro street features in the three major magazines by 1998, the fat tire look was still popular in Du Quoin as evidenced by this '59 Caddy (left) and Dave VerSchave's ultra trick '66 Nova.*
Butch Pate photos

### Black Barge
*This huge pro street Cadillac (right) was originally built by Mark Grimes. It was featured in the February '94 issue of* Hot Rod *and the October '94 issue of* Popular Hot Rodding.
Butch Pate photo

**Pro Street Persistence**
Steve Gantz's slick '65 Corvette (left) and Kenny & Angie Davis's '55 Bel Air (above) roamed the Fairgrounds in 1998. *Butch Pate photos*

Bob Maynard's Camaro is shot for Hot Rod Magazine (right)
*Marc Telder photo*

### In the Weeds
*Johnny Young's '60 Starliner (right) was one of the stars of the '98 show. Several other potent pro street builds were there, too. Wally Elder's Daytona (bottom) was a hit at the 1991 Nats.*

*Butch Pate photos*

Marc Telder photo

161

**Who You Callin' Strange?**
*A still wet-behind-the-ears Tim Strange brought out this crazy Hemi-powered DeSoto, (right) a fan favorite in '98.* Butch Pate photos

162

### Rip Roarin' Good Times
*Participants and fans either didn't know or didn't show that the Street Machine Nationals had been booted from Du Quoin after the '98 show, because there was plenty of fun to be had both on the grounds and off.*

Butch Pate photos

165

167

**Buckles Up...**
*Gary Buckles' groundbreaking (and ground scraping) '71 Camaro (left) debuted in 1994 and was a fan favorite in Du Quoin.*
*John Jackson/NotStock Photography photos*

**R 'Dem Bones?**
Todd Clark's Camaro sported some of the coolest graphics known to man, expertly applied by pro street legend Scott Sullivan. It wowed the crowd in Du Quoin first in 1993.

Todd Clark photos provided

# chapter 9

## THE BUSINESS
### RICH GEBHARDT

James Brooks photo

# chapter 9 | THE BUSINESS

### Dragstrip Pedal-er

You've got to like drag racing in order to ride your bike just to watch. You've got to *love* drag racing in order to ride that same bike 15 miles one way every weekend. It is no stretch to say that as a kid, young Rich Gebhardt *really loved* drag racing. Some things haven't changed a bit.

"When I was younger, my brother was into cars. We had a little dragstrip in Beardstown, about 15 miles west of my hometown of Virginia, Illinois," Gebhardt recalled. "My brother lived there, and sometimes I'd stay with him on the weekends and he'd take me. Otherwise, I rode my bike from home," he said.[1]

All that pedaling must have made Gebhardt yearn for the days when he could mash the loud pedal on a high performance ride of his own, because the prolific chassis specialist has seemingly been cranking out one incredible car after the next ever since. His first feature car appeared in *Popular Hot Rodding* in 1986.[2] Since then, he's built more pro street cars and race cars than he can remember and is second only to Scott Sullivan in total number of feature cars from the Street Machine Nationals era of 1977-2000 (in case you were wondering, Sullivan has 34 while Gebhardt has 25). And while business as of late has focused almost exclusively on dragstrip-only cars, there is no question the self-taught fabrication master was once a major player in the pro street game.

## Open For Business

While Gebhardt may have gotten his start working on cars with his brother out at the strip in Beardstown, his first paying gig turning wrenches was at Jack's Auto Clinic in Jacksonville, Illinois.[3] The shop was owned by Rich's girlfriend at the time, former wife Jacklyn. One day, Jack noticed Rich's car in front of his home—broken down with a busted Powerglide. Within three hours, it was gone. When Jack discovered Gebhardt had completed the job himself with no power tools, he offered the young gearhead a job. He accepted.

Throughout his high school years, Gebhardt continued to work on cars and build his skills. However, it could be said that if not for some shoddy hired help, the world of the Street Machine Nationals might have never heard of him. His first attempt at a pro streeter was a big block Chevy powered 1982 Monte Carlo with a tunnel ram and Enderle injection. Gebhardt got the idea for the car after seeing Warren Johnson's pro stocker running on the NHRA circuit. He farmed out the chassis work and was horrified with the hack job that returned.

"I was about 19 or 20, and when I saw WJ's car, I thought it was the coolest thing," he recalled. "I found one in a salvage yard that had been burned up under the hood. I saved up all the money I had, which wasn't much, and took it to a guy and had it built," he said.[1] "It was terrible. I ended up cutting it all apart, bought a welder, and fabricated it up right," he added. It would be the first of many such builds to come.

The unassuming Gebhardt can be credited with jumping in—along with Rick Dobbertin and Rocky Robertson—to kick off the trend to use a late-model front wheel drive car as a starting point for a wild pro street car. Gebhardt's second feature car—a radical 1986 Chevy Cavalier—snagged the cover as well as a full feature in the November '86 issue of *Popular Hot Rodding*.[4] The car had started life as an Avis rental.[4] Gebhardt built a full tube chassis for the little Chevy and swapped the drivetrain over from the Monte Carlo, now even more potent in the lighter Cavalier. The car would later be featured in *Hot Rod*, as well.[5]

172

## chapter 9 | THE BUSINESS

When Chevy brass saw the car in *PHR*, they invited Gebhardt to display it in the GM booth at the 1987 SEMA show in Vegas. "They actually flew some people down. They looked at the car, then they made me a deal," he recounted. The trendsetting ride was hauled to the show and Rich and his wife were paid a negotiated fee and then flown to Vegas, all on Chevy's dime. The wicked blue Z24 appeared in the booth along with another custom Chevy owned by famed slugger Reggie Jackson.[4]

In addition to the drivetrain, Gebhardt also transferred the personalized license plate from the Monte to the Cavalier. *PHR* must have really liked it. The descriptive tag served as the feature title for both cars, making Gebhardt the only street machiner in history to have two different cars featured in the same magazine in the same year in which both article titles were the same.[2,4]

On the heels of two different features on his own builds in 1986, Gebhardt was increasingly being asked to do chassis and suspension work for others. In 1987, he decided to leave his job at Jack's and set off on his own, opening Gebhardt's Pro Street Cars & Performance Center in Jacksonville, Illinois. The timing could not have been better. By that time, over half (51.39%) of all cars featured in *Car Craft* were of the tubbed variety.[6] *Hot Rod* and *Popular Hot Rodding* were just behind at nearly one in three (31.62% and 31,73%, respectively). By the early '90s, all three major magazines would be greater than 50% pro street composition and no one was better situated to capitalize on the boom than Gebhardt.

Without a doubt, the Z24 had been a smashing success. However, it was Gebhardt's next car—a 1989 Beretta—that secured his place in history. The car debuted at the '89 Street Machine Nationals in Du Quoin and managed to earn both third place in Best Pro Street and, more surprisingly, Grand Champion/Best Overall Street Machine.[7] The award was no small feat, as Scott Sullivan's '55 Chevy, Matt & Debbie Hay's Thunderbird, Mike Adams' '66 Nova, and Tom Davis' Sullivan-painted Beretta all took runners-up.[7] Despite the quality and depth of the field, the orange-hued Chevy was a bit of a long-shot upset to win. It also garnered Hot Rod Top Ten of the Year honors.[8]

*173*

"It was a total surprise, I mean it was a cool car and all—all aluminum V6 and a Lenco—but as far as pro street, I guess it was definitely what they were looking for," he said. With Gebhardt doing all the heavy fabrication work and former wife Jacklyn doing much of the tin and finish work, the car represented a classic pro stock look applied to the brand new and then-ultra-hot Beretta body style. The couple's goal with the car was to finish in the Top Five GM category at Du Quoin, so the strong showing in the people's choice category came as a total shock.[9]

Gebhardt's cars could always be described as heavy on the "pro" and light on the "street," and to this day, he's perfectly fine with that. "I've always been more of a race car guy," he admits. "It got to the point where they were looking for more amenities and such for driving on the street, but I've always been more into full chassis cars with aluminum interiors and all that stuff. That's what I always liked," he added.

### Do Ones For Others

The steady march from feature car to cover car to Hot Rod Top Ten of the Year and Grand Champion at the Street Machine Nationals in just three years had certainly brought Gebhardt a great deal of exposure and notoriety. At the same time, having a first-of-its kind shop dedicated to anything from phone tech support to turn-key custom street cars didn't hurt, either.[10] As business geared up, the now legendary fabricator would find himself increasingly busy. And while a total of 11 different cars would go on to be featured 15 times over the next four years, Gebhardt would never again be listed as the owner of a magazine feature-quality car.[10]

The first such car was a wild pro street Ford Tempo built for fellow Illinoisan Bob Northrop. The low-slung alternative body style car debuted in Du Quoin in '88 and was first featured in *Car Craft* in July 1989.[11] It featured all the typical Gebhardt tricks, including a full tube chassis and clean sheet metal work under the hood and in the interior. Before being featured in *Hot Rod*, the car placed third at the '89 Nats in Best Ford.[7,12]

## chapter 9 | THE BUSINESS

Northrop's Ford would prove to be the last non-GM product Gebhardt would ever build that would be featured in one of the big three car magazines. The first in a litany of potent Generals was Rick Cox's 1988 Cavalier. The car again featured a full tube chassis and a tunnel-ram with Enderle injection reminiscent of Gebhardt's own Z24 built four years prior. Despite its wicked stance and excellent craftsmanship, the car was crowded off the podium in '89 at the Nats by the likes of Robertson, Trepanier, Sullivan, and Hay.[7]

When initially featured, the car sported a simple red monochrome paint job.[13] After the near miss in '89, Cox went back to the drawing board and further refined the car for the '90 Nats. Cox scrapped the injection for a more traditional single Holley dominator, and although the unmistakable Scott Sullivan shredded-metal graphics and refined induction system certainly added to the car's appeal, it again failed to place in 1990.[13,14]

Gebhardt must have been a busy guy in 1989, because yet another high-end car of his creation landed ink in early 1990. Showing variations on a Beretta theme, Gebhardt constructed yet another 1989 model, this time for customer Charles Anderson.[15] The slick blue full tube chassis car demonstrated a move toward streetability for Gebhardt, as it incorporated a carpeted, non-rattling aluminum interior and a fully dressed, well-mannered 350 cubic inch tuned port motor.[15] Subtle and clean as it was, it was likely underappreciated due to a glut of pro street Berettas that all debuted around the same time.

When Gebhardt Pro Street Cars employee (and Gebhardt's brother-in-law at the time) Jimmy Weishaar decided he wanted to build a car of his own in 1990, he decided to do what his boss had done at the very beginning.[10] Namely, he emulated a Warren Johnson pro stock car as the starting point for a wild and potent pro streeter. However, WJ was no longer driving a Chevy Monte Carlo but rather an Oldsmobile Cutlass.

The team initially wanted to keep the car an all-Oldsmobile affair, but with no viable Olds powerplant available, they settled on a 468 big block Chevy instead.[10] The car was a hit at the '90 Street Machine Nationals, taking second place behind Troy Trepanier's Pro Box Impala in Best Engi-

neered, third in Best GM behind Trepanier and Al Hinds' Beretta, and runner up in Grand Champion Street Machine.[16] The car was later featured in *Car Craft*, *Popular Hot Rodding*, and *Hot Rod* magazines, garnering a small cover spot on *PHR*.[17-19]

After Jeff Carter's Gebhardt-built '88 Camaro landed in *Car Craft* in April '92, Gebhardt's count of feature-caliber pro street builds was up to nine.[6,20] However, up to that point, the oldest car in the bunch had been Gebhardt's first, the 1982 Chevy Monte Carlo. All that changed in a big way at the Street Machine Nationals in 1992 with the debut of Mike Lloyd's Gebhardt-built pro-mod style purple '72 GTO. The car featured award-winning Kim Shirley-applied paint and graphics, taking first place in best Paint and Graphics in the Pro Engineered category in Du Quoin.[21,22]

The car featured one of the first enormous pro-mod style rear wings employed on a street car and a twin Holley Dominator and NOS induction system. It was featured in all three major magazines within one month of the show, marking the last such car Gebhardt built during the pro street era.[21,23]

While the car was built to be a strong performer, like so many other cars, in the mad dash to get it done in time for Du Quoin, it was still largely unsorted. When it was tested the day after the show, it was the only pro street car that failed to post a full pass under power down the nearby eighth-mile I-57 drag strip.

Gebhardt then built a series of late model GM products for late-to-the-party pro street builders Merle and Jack Goldesberry. The first—Merle's '93 Pontiac Grand Am—had a blown small block Chevy and the requisite Gebhardt full tube chassis.[24] That build was followed up by Jack's Cavalier Z24, an '89 in orange with a tunnel ram.[25] The last Gebhardt/Goldesberry collaboration proved to be the first-ever pro street fourth generation Trans Am, Merle's radical B&M Megablown '94. The groundbreaking car featured the first roots-blown LT1 engine ever.[26]

Merle Goldesberry's final pro street car, a 1996 Pontiac Sunfire, proved to be the last big-tired, full tube chassis car ever featured in *Car Craft*—at least for now. However, Gebhardt did not assist in its construction.[27]

176

The final Gebhardt-built car to be featured in a magazine was Jay and Susan Osman's screaming yellow '93 Pontiac Grand Prix.[28] After nearly a decade at the pinnacle of pro street, Gebhardt ultimately transitioned into a "more go and less show" approach. Nevertheless, his place in pro street history is secure.

### *Gebhardt Pro Cars Loses the Street*

Gebhardt is satisfied with the impressive list of builds to his credit. But, according to him, he was nowhere near finished building cars when the magazine coverage dried up in the early to mid '90s. Recognizing the fact that pro streeters seemed to be a dying breed and wishing to maintain profitability in his business, he shortened the name of the shop to Gebhardt's Pro Cars in 1998. Although he says the shop still builds back-half and tube chassis street cars regularly, demand is nothing like it once was. Instead, the vast majority of his cars today are intended for drag racing applications exclusively.

"I have always seemed to have at least one pro street car going," he said. Most recently, he has started construction on a pro street 2012 Camaro for one brave customer. However, fans shouldn't expect to see a large number of new builds from Gebhardt any time in the future.

"I'm 51 years old. I am really kind of winding down," he said reluctantly. "I have been doing this a long, long time and it is hard to make any money—especially now in this economy. And if you are doing it on your own, it is even harder to turn stuff around fast enough to keep people happy," he concluded.

When asked about his recollections of the Street Machine Nationals, Gebhardt admitted that he enjoyed the show and the camaraderie that developed among the big builders of the day. He still has his '89 Grand Champion Super Bowl-style ring, and although he never had it sized in order to actually wear it, it still makes for a great conversation piece.

When asked specifically about Du Quoin, Gebhardt was similarly positive. "It [Du Quoin] seemed a lot more laid back and spread out than other

shows," he said. "It was just a real nice setting with the lake and all that. After a hard thrash to finish a build, we always went down there to kind of unwind," he added assuredly.

With an impressive line of incredible cars that helped populate fairgrounds and dragstrips across the nation throughout the late '80s and early '90s, one thing about Rich Gebhardt is certain. It is lucky for all of us that the so-called "chassis guy" he hired to complete that first Monte Carlo way back in 1985 was a low talent hack—or at the very least did a bad job on the would-be magazine car. If he hadn't, Gebhardt might have left well enough alone and the entire street machine scene would have been worse off because of it.

## References

1. Gebhardt R. Custom car builder. Personal communication: Telephone interview. April 11, 2012.
2. McGowan J. PD Quick. *Popular Hot Rodding*. January 1986:42-44.
3. McGowan J. Hi-Risers: Rich & Jacklyn Gebhardt. *Car Craft*. April 1990:14-15.
4. Losee J. Pretty Darn Quick. *Popular Hot Rodding*. November 1986:40-41; 82.
5. Baskerville G. Z-Wiz. *Hot Rod*. December 1986:56-57.
6. Brooks T. Street Machine Nationals magazine research database; *Car Craft, Hot Rod*, and *Popular Hot Rodding*; 1977-2000. 2013.
7. Pitt J. The Best Ever! Street Machine Nationals. *Car Craft*. October 1989:21-32.
8. Baskerville G. Hot Rod Magazine's 1989 Top Ten. *Hot Rod*. December 1989:26-29.
9. Baskerville G. Ballistic Beretta. *Hot Rod*. October 1989:64-65.
10. Baechtel J. The Pro Shop. *Hot Rod*. April 1990:87-91.
11. Dahlquist S. Tempo-Rary Insanity. *Hot Rod*. July 1989:89-90.
12. Bernsau T. Quickening Tempo. *Car Craft*. July 1989:46-47.
13. Losee J. Pro-Gressive. *Car Craft*. February 1990:122-123.
14. Baechtel J. Red Menace. *Car Craft*. January 1991:80-81.
15. Fetherston D. Tuned Port Terror. *Popular Hot Rodding*. April 1990:28-29.
16. Rathbun C. Street Machine Nats '90. *Car Craft*. October 1990:18-43.
17. Fetherston D. Oh So Bad. *Popular Hot Rodding*. October 1990:52-53; 110.
18. Rathbun C. Pro Archetype. *Car Craft*. March 1991:84-85.

19. Baskerville G. Street Slasher Supreme. *Hot Rod*. November 1990:86-87.
20. Killeen S. Factory Fresh. *Car Craft*. April 1992:72-73.
21. Anderson S. True Believer. *Hot Rod*. October 1992:50-52.
22. Baechtel J. Show of Force. *Car Craft*. October 1992:18-30.
23. Baechtel J. Purple Haze. *Car Craft*. November 1992:80-83.
24. Kaya B. Warning Sign. *Car Craft*. December 1993:36-38.
25. Kaya B. Cavalier Attitude. *Car Craft*. February 1994:56-57.
26. Cook M. Good as Gold. *Car Craft*. November 1994:58-59.
27. Cook M. Sun Inferno. *Car Craft*. March 1996:54-56.
28. Fetherston D. Poncho Cheese. *Popular Hot Rodding*. December 1994:94-95.

# chapter 10

# INDELIBLE MARK
## MARK GRIMES

## chapter 10 | INDELIBLE MARK

### *Keeping Up with the Andersons*

Before Mark Grimes could even legally drive a car, he had his heart set on racing one. The Omaha, Nebraska, native has been hunkered over the fenders of anything with wheels in an effort to make it perform better for as long as he can remember. Eventually a pro street hero, Grimes is quick to point out that if not for some straight-line gearheads in his neighborhood during his youth, he likely would never have ascended the ranks of the fat tired elite in the '80s and '90s.

"When I was very young, I grew up next to a family—the Andersons—who loved to drag race," he said. "Their dad, Fred, had a pro stock '57 Chevy way back in the early '70s and he would pull wheelies out on the street. It would just blow my mind," he recalled.[1] Those memories of roasting tires and high horsepower would serve young Grimes well in the future.

Never content to simply watch the neighbors have all the fun, young Mark did the same as many of his future pro street contemporaries—he built models. More specifically, Grimes would kit bash several models, using the coolest parts and pieces from each kit to build the wildest creations imaginable. Even though he couldn't yet drive a real car, he relentlessly planned and plotted, cut and molded, and glued and sanded his plastic miniature visions into reality.

However, the creative juices in quarter scale were marinating deep into his soul. It wasn't long before the future pro street hero was concocting creations all his own in full size.

### Hot for Tubs

"When I finally grew up and started building real cars, I was fortunate enough to have friends with welders and other tools, and I learned to do a lot of the fabrication work myself," Grimes said. A chance encounter with a speed shop owner in Texas while Grimes was away at Lubbock Christian College resulted in his first exposure to a tubbed car on the street. He absolutely loved the look. The pro street bug had bitten hard, and Grimes would never be the same.

At the time, he was driving a gold 1970 Monte Carlo with the widest Centerlines he could stuff inside the factory wheel wells. However, the combination of the local Lubbock pro street mentor and magazine coverage of Scott Sullivan's '67 Nova had him ready to grab a torch and take the plunge into the tubbed brotherhood. But, as so often happens, life dictated otherwise.

"I was still in college and didn't have any money. I met my soon-to-be wife Diana, a motor head herself, and we got married," Grimes reflected. "But it was a few more years before I was in a position to build the kind of car I really wanted to," he said.

Following his college graduation and wedding to Diana, Grimes purchased a Camaro and started building the car to take to some local shows. Although he managed to successfully install a used blower on the car, it still sported a factory rear suspension. It would be two more years before he laid claim to his first tubbed car.

"I was attending the Hot Rod Supernats in Indy and I traded for a tubbed, ex-racecar Chevette," Grimes said. After getting the car back home to Nebraska, he completely tore it apart with the help of friends Jay Thompson and John Jacobsen. The car was detailed, painted red, and equipped with a 6-71 supercharger. "That was my first pro street car, and after that I was completely hooked," he admitted.

Grimes took the car to a number of shows in 1981 and 1982 and was thrilled at fans' response to his homebuilt bad-boy Chevette. "People were going crazy over this little car, and I was absolutely loving it," he recounted.

"I couldn't get rid of it fast enough so that I could get started on another one," he said.

By September 1983, Grimes' second effort, a tubbed and blown 1972 Chevy Vega, appeared in *Hot Rod*'s event coverage of the '83 Street Machine Nationals.[2] The ice blue, big-block stuffed rocket was a modest success, earning a full-color feature in both *Popular Hot Rodding* and *Car Craft*.[3,4] The clean and well executed Chevy had helped Grimes start to make a name for himself, but it would be his next creation that put him on the map for good in 1986.

### *America's Best Street Machine*

Just in time for the newly-relocated Street Machine Nationals in Du Quoin in 1986, Grimes unveiled his ultra-clean 1965 Malibu to the delight of the swelling mass of pro street faithful. The car was an instant success, earning second place in Best Street Machine, first place in Best Interior, and second place in Best Engine at the 1986 show.[5] The car featured suicide doors, a chromed and narrowed Ford nine-inch rear, a blown and injected big block, and a silky smooth ice-blue candy pearl paint job.[6,7] Fellow pro street builder Scott Sullivan loved the color, admitting that it was exactly the hue he was initially going for on his '67 Nova. Only Dobbertin's J-2000 out-pointed the 'Bu for Best Street Machine and Best Engine at the Nats.

Ironically, the only major magazine that failed to feature the car in 1986 heralded it as "America's Best Street Machine" by 1987.[8] After a light refresh, Grimes had treated the car to subtle graphics, new tires, an altered grille, and a few other refinements. However, it was good enough to slide the build up to first place in Best Overall Street Machine for the '87 Nats as part of the street machine "triple crown." The car also took first place in Best Interior, second place in Best Engineered, and third place in Best Engine.[9]

"I was building the car in 1985 and my first son was born June 25th, 1985. Guess what else was happening that weekend? The Street Machine Nationals!" Grimes quipped with a laugh. Attending to obviously more pressing family matters, Grimes was unable to attend the show. After de-

buting the car in 1986, he admits he rightfully placed behind Dobbertin's J-2000 with the Malibu in '86. "It was completely understandable. Rick's J-2000 was mind-boggling—head over heels over my car. No doubt about it," he added.

At the first major national event of the '87 show season, the Hot Rod Supernationals, acquaintance Robby Bennett approached Grimes about purchasing the car. Grimes didn't think much of the request at the time, figuring young Bennett—several years Grimes' junior—would likely not have the juice necessary to purchase such a high-level build.

"He was just a kid and was hanging around with us. I thought he was just talking," Grimes laughed. After a series of phone calls, Bennett had made an offer Grimes couldn't refuse. The two agreed to complete the transaction at the Street Machine Nationals; however, Grimes insisted that he would retain ownership until after the awards ceremony at the show.

"After I hung up the phone, I thought 'Yeah, right, this is a joke. No way this young kid comes up with this kind of money,'" Grimes said. However, it was no joke. An eager Bennett awaited in Du Quoin with a big sack of cash, eager and ready to buy the 'Bu.

"We pull in the gates and there's Robby with this big brown paper bag. He comes running up and says, 'Mark, take this right now! I'm scared to death I'm gonna lose all this money!'" Grimes recalled. "I looked at him and said, 'Are you serious?!'" Bennett assured Grimes he was indeed serious. Grimes retained the car through the weekend, earned the Grand Champion ring, and handed Bennett the keys on Sunday afternoon.[1]

As *Car Craft* staffer Brian Hatano would later describe the ever-growing stakes in the pro street competition, "Grimes not only placed himself at center stage, but he's also entered a serious contest of one-upmanship among an elite clan of super-talented and definitely fanatical car builders who have added what we can only describe as a fantasy dimension to the hobby of car crafting."[8] Grimes' next version of that "fantasy dimension" would be even wilder than anything else he had ever created.

## *Overblown*

Grimes drove home from Du Quoin in '87 empty-trailered and nearly in tears. He spent mile after excruciating mile back to Omaha wondering if he had done the right thing in selling his prized Malibu. With a sack full of Benjamin Franklins in hand, he started plotting his next build.

"Between Rick's J-2000 and Matt and Debbie Hays' Olds' and so many other guys who took front wheel drive cars and made them into wild pro streeters, I decided to do something similar for my next car," he said. However, the specific model to use as a starting point remained a mystery until a quick trip to the local Chevy dealership revealed a banged up little Chevy Celebrity.

"I went to pick up my Suburban that was in for service and I noticed this black Celebrity Eurosport with the front end punched in the corner," Grimes recounted. Eager to unload the car, the dealer offered to sell the whole thing as-is for just $1,000. Grimes gladly accepted. He took the car directly to friend John Jacobsen of Jacobsen Racing, and the next build was on.

Grimes knew from the very beginning that the car would be a full tube chassis construction with a big block Chevy, aiming it from the start at the upper echelon of pro street. What he hadn't yet settled on was an induction system. After seeing a friend's wild Harley Davidson with a B&M mini-blower hanging off the side of the engine, he started thinking about some new possibilities. "I looked at that Harley, then I remembered Rick's Nova with the twin turbos feeding up into the bug catcher. From there it was simple. I just *had* to do three blowers," he said.

Groundbreaking as it was, the Eurosport faced tough competition in its debut in 1988. Matt and Debbie Hays' Thunderbird, Scott Sullivan's '55 Chevy, and Rocky Robertson's LeSabre all posed formidable threats. By the end of the '88 Nats, Grimes had garnered first place in Best Supercharged Vehicle, second place in Best Pro Street and Best General Motors, third place in Best Engine Compartment, and runner-up for Best Overall Street Machine.[10]

In addition to the wild thrice-blown big block, the car featured a number of other firsts, as well. A cool child's seat complete with five-point racing harness had been mounted between the huge rear tubs for the Grimes' then-infant son Damon.[11,12] Ferrari Testarossa mirrors and Corvette taillights headlined a number of unique body mods. Perhaps most impressive, the entire car had been built in just 10 months.

The Monday after the '88 Nats, the Eurosport proved its mettle, making a number of passes down the eighth-mile strip in nearby Benton to verify that it had a little "go" to back up its triple-huffed "show."[13] After thousands of hours of prep and construction and an incredible outlay of cash, the only question *Car Craft* could muster was "What will come out of Grimes' garage next?" Such was life for the pro street elite in the world of what-have-you-done-for-me-lately street machining. Originally debuted at the 1988 Hot Rod Supernationals, the car had been out for a total of 24 days at the time of the test.[14]

### Life After Pro Street

The Eurosport marked four straight pro street builds for the innovative Nebraskan. By 1992, though, he opted to take a turn in another direction altogether. Grimes expertly pieced together a sleek pro-touring style '62 Nova in just five weeks—just in time for the summer show season.[15] The subtle pearl green cruiser had an electronic fuel injected 4.3 liter V-6 and then-monstrous 17-inch Boyd's wheels.[16] The car was groundbreaking enough to land a prestigious Hot Rod Top Ten, ironically a feat none of Grimes' previous—and far more costly—builds had ever accomplished.

Grimes' last car ever featured in the big three magazines—at least for now—was a cool 1968 pro street Cadillac convertible. Close friend Brad Fanshaw, a fellow Omaha native and founder of bonspeed wheels, remembers the car well. "That car was an absolute blast. It was huge and with the drop top and huge tires, we cruised many a fairground in that thing," Fanshaw recounted.[17]

Again breaking new ground in functional, well-mannered street machines, the "Black Barge" featured a Holley fuel injected 510 cubic inch Cadillac powerplant, 15-inch wide rear meats, and a flawless black paintjob.[18] The car was so massive that the typical huge rear wheel tubs didn't even make a dent in the passenger area, leaving room for a full rear seat the size of a small sofa.[19] It was the perfect fun cruiser that had plenty of room for all Grimes' friends. And maybe even a few of their friends, too.

By the time the Caddy hit the streets in 1994, much of the pro street popularity wave that had elevated Grimes and his contemporaries to near rock-star status had died out. In its place, the pro-touring movement that Grimes' little Nova had foreshadowed had taken center stage. However, there is no question that Grimes' eclectic mix of classic muscle cars, cutting edge late-models, and always-cool customs had left an indelible mark on the street machine scene.

Grimes recalls the Street Machine Nationals with fondness, proudly claiming Du Quoin as one of the best venues ever. "The grounds were outstanding. You couldn't find a better place for a car show," he said. In particular, he remembers the early set-up on Thursdays with the rest of his pro street elite fraternity brothers as a notable high point. "That just set the tone for the whole weekend. Just one cool car after another came rolling in and you just *knew* it was coming," he added.

When asked which car of all his legendary builds is his favorite, Grimes answers without hesitation. "The Malibu. I told Robby when I sold it to him to call me first before he sold it to anyone else because I wanted it back," Grimes said assuredly.

Sure enough, 11 years later Bennett needed to sell the car in order to buy a house. He tracked Grimes down and offered to reunite the car with its original builder. A deal was struck and the car once deemed "America's Best Street Machine" was headed back to Grimes' garage.

Grimes operated MAG Motoring for several years and built a number of cars for customers from his shop in Omaha. The venture was a welcome aside to Grimes' long-held family business of providing money handling machines and services to financial institutions. However, work responsibilities ultimately squeezed Grimes for time, resulting in MAG's closure in 2009.

At the same time, Grimes never stopped building cars for himself and his sons, now grown with families of their own. Most recently, the trio has dusted the cobwebs off the Malibu and plans to show the car at the 2013 Street Machine Nationals and a number of other shows. Grandson Paxton (like the supercharger) has already claimed dibs on the infant racing seat once occupied by his dad Damon.

The Malibu is back and better than ever with a more streetable EFI system perched atop the blower. But don't think you can just show up in Du Quoin with a wadded brown sack full of hundreds and whisk the car away. Grimes insists he won't make that mistake twice.

Not for any amount that would fit in just one bag, at least.

## References

1. Grimes M. Custom car builder. Personal communication: Telephone interview. May 27, 2011.
2. Ganahl P, Baechtel J, Baskerville G, Davis M. Street Machine Nationals '83: Still Smokin'. *Hot Rod*. September 1983:60-64.
3. Hall A. Great Plains Drifters. *Popular Hot Rodding*. November 1983:22-26.
4. Asher J. Azure Like It. *Car Craft*. January 1985:56-57.
5. Anand D. Street Machine Nationals. *Car Craft*. October 1986:23-32.
6. Losee J. Pro One. *Popular Hot Rodding*. October 1986:46-49.
7. Baskerville G. Maliblue Thunder. *Hot Rod*. November 1986:126-127.
8. Hatano B. America's Best Street Machine? *Car Craft*. December 1997:20-24.
9. Bernsau T. Street Machine Nationals. *Car Craft*. October 1987:32-45.
10. Pitt J. Heat Machine Nationals. *Car Craft*. October 1988:16-27.
11. Hemer C. Overblown. *Popular Hot Rodding*. October 1988:56-57; 97; 96.
12. Baskerville G. Red, White & Blown. *Hot Rod*. October 1988:91-92.
13. Hatano B. Kings of Pro Street. *Car Craft*. November 1988:18-28.
14. Baskerville G. Supernationals 10. *Hot Rod*. September 1988:25-36.
15. Smith J. It's Hip to be Square. *Hot Rod*. March 1993:67-72.
16. Baechtel J. Nouveau Nova. *Car Craft*. October 1992:90-91.
17. Fanshaw B. Founder and CEO, Bonneville Worldwide, Inc. Personal communication: Telephone interview. March 13, 2013.
18. Freiburger D. Preview of Caddy Attractions. *Hot Rod*. February 1994:38.
19. Fetherston D. Black Barge. *Popular Hot Rodding*. October 1994:42-43.

# chapter 11
## NOTHIN' BUT A GOOD TIME
### THE PARTY HEATS UP
### 1990-1993

Butch Pate photo

## chapter 11 | NOTHIN' BUT A GOOD TIME

*Not a dime, I can't pay my rent*
*I can barely make it through the week*
*Saturday night I'd like to make my girl*
*But right now I can't make ends meet*

*I'm always workin' slavin' every day*
*Gotta get away from that same old same old*
*I need a chance just to get away*
*If you could hear me think this is what I'd say*

*Don't need nothin' but a good time*
*How can I resist*
*Ain't lookin' for nothin' but a good time*
*And it don't get better than this*

"Nothin' But a Good Time," by Bobby Dall, Bret Michaels, Bruce Johanneson, Bruce Anthony, and Rikki Rocket; © copyright 1988, Universal Music Publishing Group[1]

### Fast Livin' in the Nineties

Prior to 1990, the Street Machine Nationals' longest tenure in any town had been its first five years in Indy. A combination of a cramped facility and too many run-ins with the law led to the show's departure in '81. After three years in Springfield, followed by just one year in East St. Louis, the show had settled in quaint Du Quoin for what seemed like a match made in heaven. To a growing mass of concerned local citizens, it sure felt like three days of hell every year.

By 1990, the Nats had become a full-blown car show franchise, boasting a total of six events spread across three months and two time zones.[2] None of the other five regional events came close in size or spectacle to THE Street Machine Nationals in Du Quoin, though. With stops in Florida, Michigan, Indiana, New York, and Missouri to serve as bridesmaids to the Big Dance in Illinois, the event enjoyed widespread appeal from "car guys" and random partiers alike.

Media attention for the show remained significant in 1990, with *Car Craft* and *Hot Rod*—both owned by Petersen Publishing—devoting more than six pages each to event coverage.[3,4] Although *Popular Hot Rodding*—owned by competing McMullen Argus Publications—did not publish formal event coverage, staffers were still in attendance to shoot features. Other stateside niche publications such as *Super Chevy* and *Super Ford* and a host of foreign magazines also attended to gather feature content, too.

Former Family Events Marketing Director Susan Davis recalled the unique coverage she had helped facilitate early in the Du Quoin years. "ESPN was still relatively new and they were looking for things to fill airtime. They actually came to Du Quoin and covered the event," she said.[5] "We got a lot of national media attention just because it was still kind of a curiosity," she added. The legend of the Nats was growing.

The big winner in '90 was undoubtedly Troy Trepanier's 1960 mint green Impala. The car took Best Paint, Best Engineered, Best Interior, Best GM, and Grand Champion Street Machine.[4] Rocky Robertson's refreshed LeSabre took Best Pro Street. Other notables included the '90 Oldsmobile of Gebhart Pro Street Cars' Jimmy Weishaar, the Beretta of Al Hinds, the Scott Sullivan-painted '56 Chevy Pickup of John Spreitzer, and the peach '51 Nash of Johnny Young.[4] Neon colors and hot scallops seemed to be the flavor of the month.[3]

Attendance proved excellent, with more than 106,000 spectators and 3,600 cars on site, both of which were Du Quoin bests. Not all was rosy, though. Despite positive press in the national magazines, a growing chorus of locals voiced concern about the show.

One resident who asked to remain anonymous told the *Du Quoin Evening Call* that he "feared for his life" and that those who spoke favorably of the event "must not have seen the cars running over nicely manicured lawns, and they did not have to endure the fear that someone would throw a brick through their window."[6] Another stated that he personally witnessed "people defecating and urinating in yards, young women exposing themselves, and all the debris, cans, and beer containers which were strewn about town."[6]

That trash would later become a point of contention between the fairgrounds and the event organizers. Jeff Mason, a 30+ year staff member at the DSF, recalled the tremendous volume of refuse created by the crowd on the fairgrounds alone, not to mention what was left around town. "At the peak of the show, we had three 20 yard roll-offs a day and a crew of around 15 people going all the time just to keep up," Mason said.[7] For reference, over the three days of the show, that's roughly the equivalent of nine school buses full of garbage picked up just on the fairgrounds.

Although significant, the volume wasn't anything Mason and his crew couldn't handle. "We got so efficient that after a few years, we would have all the trash out of the facility, all the streets flushed with Pine-Sol, and all the restrooms cleaned and sanitized within three hours," he added. Unfortunately for Du Quoin residents, the same wasn't true of the mess on the city's streets.

As longtime *Du Quoin Evening Call* Publisher John Croessman described it, "It's a four mile Friday night cruise from the Du Quoin State Fair into the City of Du Quoin that lasts for three days. It's beer cans everywhere. It's full coolers and empty heads taken over by a 'Show 'n Shine' mentality," he wrote.[8]

Retired Illinois State Trooper and lifelong Du Quoin resident Marc Melvin worked every Nats event in his hometown except the first in 1986. "I was a junior trooper and they assigned me to patrol some backwoods area of Randolph County for some inexplicable reason," he remembered.[9] The Sergeant and eventual Master Sergeant wasn't so fortunate from then on, being assigned to duty at the event each year from 1987-1998.

"The amount of trash was just indescribable. You could just walk along afterwards and you could see where people had been gathered by the depths of the trash that had been pushed out," Melvin said. Serving on the tactical team, Mason's primary assignment was to work the Walmart & Southtown Shopping Center. "I was assigned to the epicenter of this disaster. All the stores would close except for Walmart—they would stay open long enough to sell out of bleach and beer—but the other places really couldn't conduct business," he added.

Melvin had a point. For all the talk of the huge economic impact on the area, its benefits were highly concentrated to just a few businesses. Sure, hotels were full for nearly 60 miles in all directions from the fairgrounds. State police officers alone injected $15,000 into the economy for lodging on the weekend.[10] Lines at McDonalds were sometimes 30 deep, and Walmart and Kroger seemed to do well, too. But for many local businesses, the whole rowdy, congested mess was more of a hindrance than a help to their bottom line.

"Many of our local business owners really dreaded that show," recounted lifelong Du Quoin resident Fred Huff.[11] "They would actually have to close for the weekend," he added. A number of merchants in the Southtown area would even board their windows for fear that the crowd—traditionally most unruly on Saturday night—might resort to violence or vandalism.

As reported by the *Evening Call*, Illinois State Police issued 67 total citations in 1990.[12] That might seem bad enough, but consider that this total was by 9 a.m. *on Friday* (the time the gates to the show actually opened).[13] Couple that number with the 30 to 40 arrests by City of Du Quoin officers during the first day of the event and it becomes clear that trouble was brewing.[13]

By the weekend's end, Illinois State Police reported a grand total of more than 400 arrests, most of which were alcohol and traffic related. Perhaps more troubling, the state logged another 34 criminal arrests ranging from marijuana possession to disorderly conduct and weapons charges. As the *Du Quoin Evening Call* sarcastically poked, the show had been a success—"If you shut your eyes to three stabbings, naked girls, and open sewage."[14] It was far from a peaceful gathering of like-minded friends.[12]

An opinion poll conducted by the *Evening Call* following the 1990 event indicated that Du Quoin residents were against inviting the show back by a margin of around five to one.[15] Not only that, response to the poll had been tremendous. As indicated by Publisher John Croessman, "The lines were drawn largely between the people who made money from the event and the people who suffered mental or moral anguish from what went on, largely outside the gates of the Du Quoin State Fair."[15]

Despite the simmering sentiment of resentment toward the show among many locals, event promoters announced that it would return to Du Quoin for 1991.[16] And although the Nats had worn out their welcome sooner in three previous locations, the agreement meant they would be hosted for a record sixth straight year in the tiny Southern Illinois town.

## The Trend Continues

Back on the fairgrounds, 1991 proved to be the Year of Different. Perhaps spurred on by Troy Trepanier's big-finned mint green '60 Impala the year before, alternative and non-mainstream musclecar body styles were hot. At the same time, late-model converted front wheel drive cars were popular, too. Chuck Davis' orange '89 Beretta took Best Engine, Best Engineered, Best Modifications, and Best Paint. Veteran Rocky Robertson took Best Graphics and Best Interior with his LeSabre.

Relative newcomer Keith Eickert and his retina-searing pink '87 Monte Carlo pro streeter took Grand Champion and Best GM.[17] Other notables included Wally Elder's wicked '69 Dodge Daytona clone and Richard Boyd's screaming yellow '85 Camaro.

Elder's car didn't place particularly well at the '91 Nats, only managing third place in Best Mopar and second place in Best Engineered, but it was wildly popular among spectators.[17] The Daytona was front and center on the October '91 *Car Craft* and was later featured in both *Popular Hot*

*Rodding* and *Hot Rod*. With a blown and injected Hemi and a pavement-scraping stance, it was a well-executed pro street effort.

"At that time, they were actually starting to get into the pro touring thing," Elder admitted.[18] Although construction of the car commenced in 1990, the Dittmer, Missouri native didn't finish the Dodge until the summer of '91. He originally started with a 1970 Charger shell and added fiberglass reproduction pieces for the nose and huge rear wing to mimic the unmistakable Daytona body style. Toss in a nasty fire-breathing Hemi powerplant, and a full tube frame, and the end result was decidedly un-pro touring.

Other splash debuts at the show proved to be Danny Taylor's slick teal, pink, white, and black Malibu and Scott Dillingham's cool little blown V6 pro street '78 Mustang II.[19]

Perhaps the coolest happening of the weekend was the "Mild to Wild in 55 Hours" project headed up by Rick Dobbertin and a crew of who's who in pro street members. The gang braved flash flooding and nearby tornadoes and still managed to throw together a pretty cool pro street Ford pickup over the course of the weekend. *Hot Rod* staffers were within 10 feet of a lightning strike but managed to escape unscathed.[19]

Although show goer behavior was vastly improved from a year earlier, the same couldn't be said for the townsfolk of Du Quoin.

State Police had improved traffic flow with a one-way routing around the 1,500-acre plot of the Fairgrounds.[20] The city also passed ordinances to prevent glass bottles in public or camping on private lots without permission.[21] With a total of 196 State Troopers assigned to the show, officials were prepared for the worst.[22] Mayor John Rednour had successfully lobbied Special Events to pony up $5,000 to help defray the added expense for law enforcement and cleanup costs incurred by the city as a result of the event.[23]

Despite all this, it was still nearly impossible to get anywhere quickly in or around the city. The problem took center stage when ambulances couldn't get to or from the six show attendees who had been injured from the lightning strikes on the fairgrounds.

State Trooper Marc Melvin felt that in all, authorities were really beginning to understand how to best manage the crowd.[9] Du Quoin Chief of

Police Kenneth DeMent echoed this sentiment when he told the *Evening Call* that he was pleased with the '91 show. "Overall, law enforcement-wise, this was the best year we've had," he said.[24]

Amid persistent pressure to kick the show out for 1992, the Du Quoin City Council relented, voting to support its return to the DSF for a seventh straight year. Not everyone was thrilled. One resident called Mayor John Rednour prior to the Council's vote to tell him that he could "kiss her rear" if the event came back before promptly hanging up on him.[25]

## Dirty Dianna

Things seemed to be going reasonably well—at least by Nats' standards—as the show rolled back into Du Quoin for 1992. Little did anyone know that a movement was afoot by Petersen Vice President John Dianna that would eventually lead to the show's decline and ultimately contribute to its demise.

When Special Events founder Bruce Hubley purchased the rights from Petersen to host the Nats beginning in 1986, it had been a win-win for both the event promoter (Hubley) and the publication company (Petersen). The show had grown too large for a magazine publisher to effectively manage. At the same time, the editorial coverage provided by the magazines added significant value to the show, helping it to become a national draw for thousands of participants and hundreds of thousands of spectators.

It was a mutually beneficial arrangement. However, Dianna realized that his company had forfeited a substantial windfall by selling Hubley the shows. He started conjuring ways to profit directly from events again. Brazenly, he opted to cut Special Events out entirely.

In 1994, Petersen was back in the car show business. The Car Craft Summer Cruise and the Hot Rod Power Fest were born. Dianna gloated. Hubley fumed.

The '92 Nats marked one of the final years that a number of legendary pro street names would top the winner lists: Troy Trepanier's 1950 Buick taking Best Paint & Graphics, Best Engineered, Best Interior, Best

Engine, and Pro Show Class Champion.[26] Other notable builds included Al Hinds' Lumina, Chris Embree's '90 Cutlass, Frank Guidace's '72 Chevelle, and Mike Lloyd's Gebhardt-built '72 GTO. Scott Sullivan debuted his latest creation—a sinister black '57 Chevy—and Mark Grimes' subtle Nova also made the show.[27]

BF Goodrich and Linkon Auto Parts came aboard as title sponsors for '92. Both participant and spectator counts were high, just missing the Du Quoin records of 1990 by less than a few hundred. 1993 proved even more successful, eclipsing Du Quoin's best of '90 with a new record of 3,781 participants and 107,361 spectators.[28]

The cars were still cool, but virtually all the familiar names of the past had disappeared from the winner lists by 1993. Charles Anderson's two-door '92 Caprice proved to be one of the biggest winners on the weekend, snagging first place in Pro Engineered, Best Engine Compartment and Best Engineered.[29] Frank Guidace's '72 Chevelle also won big, grabbing Best Pro Street, Pro Series Grand Champion, Best Use of Plating, and Best Pro Street Engine Compartment.[29]

A number of other cars impacted the '93 installment without enjoying results on the awards podium. Local product George Norovich from West Frankfort showed up in a cool slime green pro street '55.[28] Nathan Short's neon yellow '70 Chevelle scorched eyeballs, as did Merle Goldesberry's yellow Gebhardt-built Grand Am.[28,29] Todd Clark's Scott Sullivan-immortalized "Dem Bones" Camaro also debuted.[28]

Inexplicably, Clark's Camaro won absolutely no awards on the weekend. The car featured a creamy, supple Larry Sneed street rod-style interior, a Chassis Engineering back half, and some of the most detailed graphics ever to flow from Sullivan's airbrush.[28] "That was actually my first car I ever built," Clark said.[30] A spectator each year the show had been in Du Quoin, Clark was excited to finally prowl the grounds with a ride of his own in '93.[30]

Newspaper headlines were relatively tame in the *Evening Call*'s coverage of the event. Arrests and citations were typical for the weekend both in number and severity. In fact, crowds had been a little better behaved than in the recent past. Law enforcement officials seemed convinced that their experience in handling the throng was proving beneficial. Before the end of the day on Sunday, representatives from Special Events announced that the show would be back in 1994.[31]

Little did anyone but John Dianna know that although the event would be back, it would never again be the same.

## References

1. Lyrics Freak. Nothin' But a Good Time. 2013; http://www.lyricsfreak.com/p/poison/nothin+but+a+good+time_20109986.html. Accessed May 17, 2013.
2. Bernsau T. *The Best of the Street Machine Nationals, 1972-1993*. Los Angeles, CA: Petersen Publishing Company; 1993.
3. Pettitt J. Street Dreams. *Hot Rod*. October 1990:72-78.
4. Rathbun C. Street Machine Nats '90. *Car Craft*. October 1990:18-43.
5. Davis S. Former Director, Special Events. Personal communication: Telephone interview. May 12, 2012.
6. Croessman J. Not Everyone Appreciated It. *Du Quoin Evening Call*. June 27, 1990.
7. Mason J. Executive I, Illinois Department of Agriculture, Du Quoin State Fair. Personal communication: Telephone interview. May 20, 2011.
8. Croessman J. Chrome Town, U.S.A. *Du Quoin Evening Call*. June 17, 1990: 1-2.
9. Melvin M. Illinois State Trooper (retired). Personal communication: Telephone interview. May 18, 2011.
10. Croessman J. Illinois State Police Alone Dropped $15,000 On Hotel Economy During Nationals. *Du Quoin Evening Call*. June 26, 1990.
11. Huff F. Lifelong Du Quoin resident and former Manager of the Du Quoin State Fair. Personal communication: Telephone interview. May 19, 2011.
12. Croessman J. Illinois State Police Report. *Du Quoin Evening Call*. June 25, 1990.
13. Croessman J. Show 'n Shine Ballots Cast Today at Nation's 'Hot Rod Mardi Gras'. *Du Quoin Evning Call*. June 23, 1990.
14. Croessman J. Is It Worth It? *Du Quoin Evening Call*. June 25, 1990.

15. Croessman J. The Results Are In (And Keep Coming In). *Du Quoin Evening Call*. July 20, 1990.
16. Croessman J. Street Nationals Coming Back. *Du Quoin Evening Call*. June 25, 1990.
17. Bernsau T. Street Machine Nationals. *Car Craft*. October 1991:18-31.
18. Elder W. Pro street car builder. Personal communication: Telephone interview. January 7, 2013.
19. Pettitt J. National Thrills. *Hot Rod*. October 1991:48-53.
20. Croessman J. 5,000 Flyers Help Outline Traffic Pattern During Du Quoin Street Nationals. *Du Quoin Evening Call*. June 15, 1991.
21. Petrowich T. County Targets Street Nationals with Ordinances. *Du Quoin Evening Call*. June 17, 1991.
22. Hinde JK. State Police Begin Shipping Their Own 'Street Machines' Into Region. *Du Quoin Evening Call*. June 20, 1991.
23. Croessman J. Rednour's Meeting With Street Machines Results In $5,000 Check For City. *Du Quoin Evening Call*. June 21, 1991.
24. Hinde JK. Du Quoin Police: Law Enforcementwise, Event Went Much Better This Time Around. *Du Quoin Evening Call*. June 26, 1991.
25. Croessman J. Du Quoin Council Votes for Return of Street Machine Nationals in '92. *Du Quoin Evening Call*. June 25, 1991.
26. Baechtel J. Show of Force. *Car Craft*. October 1992:18-30.
27. Anderson S. Midwest CARnival. *Hot Rod*. October 1992:42-48.
28. Kinnan R. Street Machine Nationals. *Hot Rod*. October 1993:84-87.
29. Huffman JP. 3781 Cars & Some Place To Go. *Car Craft*. October 1993:20-33.
30. Clark T. Pro street builder. Personal communication: Telephone interview. March 1, 2013.
31. Croessman J. Du Quoin Street Machine Nationals Return Next Year. *Du Quoin Evening Call*. June 28, 1993.

# chapter 12

# THE KID
# TROY TREPANIER

Annette Zimbelman photo

## chapter 12 | THE KID

### Building Junk Motors and Welding Pop Cans

**W**ho knows what young Troy Trepanier would have built as his first magazine-quality car build. The now-legendary builder inherited a clean one-owner 1966 Chevelle with a blown motor at the age of 14. His grandpa Johnny not only taught young Trepanier how to weld, but also provided the canvas the impressionable hot rodder would use to create his first masterpiece. The canvas wasn't nearly as important as the artist, though. If history is any indication, Trepanier would have done as well with just about anything with four wheels.

"My dad had an automotive shop my whole life—he actually built it when I was one—so I grew up around cars my whole life," he said.[1] "My grandfather lived on the same property as the shop and he was pipefitter and fabricator. He was one of the last craftsmen of the area that did stuff the old way," Trepanier recounted. One day when his grandfather was having trouble getting his old Chevelle to idle, he put a piece of pipe to hold the gas pedal down. Fortunately for the street machining world, the pedal went to the floor, the motor blew, and Trepanier's first car build was about to begin.[1]

With hot rodding nature flowing through his veins, Trepanier's surrounding environment help set his appointment with custom car destiny early in life. "My joke is that I grew up taking apart junk engines at my dad's shop and welding pop cans together with my grandpa, so it was the best of both worlds," he added with a laugh. Those lessons delivered to young Troy were obviously well received, as they laid the groundwork for a series of game-changing street machine and hot rod builds that continues to this day.

### A Star is LAUNCHed

The first of the line was Trepanier's aforementioned '66 Chevelle. After finishing the first version of the build, Trepanier had ordered a cool personalized license plate, "LAUNCH," in time for the '87 Nats. It was a fitting moniker for a machine that would serve as the foundation upon which the Illinois native would use to kick off an award-winning career. Prior to the now infamous engine come-apart that precipitated transfer of ownership of the Chevelle to Trepanier, he had been heavily involved in school sports in his hometown of Manteno, Illinois. He was also an avid dirt bike racer around the area. However, when the classic muscle car suddenly came into his possession, the eager 15-year old shifted gears.

"My dad and I started tinkering with it, and although he had done the local drag races and local circle track stuff, we had never built anything like (the Chevelle)," he acknowledged. The car had been treated to a Centauri red lacquer paintjob, a pro street backhalf, and a B&M blown small block when Trepanier hauled it to his first Street Machine Nationals in 1987. The effort was good enough to land him his first feature, a one-page story tucked away in the September '87 issue of *Popular Hot Rodding*—not a bad effort for a 17-year old.[2]

After seeing the plethora of wild cars and walking away from the Fairgrounds with a multi-page punch list of ideas that first year, Trepanier went back to the drawing board and retooled the car for 1988. He smoothed it out, refined key details, and made a bold color change. Out was the traditional red and chrome. In was the wild Porsche Raspberry.[3,4] *Way* in. It was slathered everywhere. Bumpers, headlight bezels, control arms, and even window trim were all liberally coated. The car looked as though it had been driven off into a river of dark Pepto Bismol, and the effect was a smash hit at the '88 Nats.

"Gray Baskerville shot the car for *Hot Rod*, and that was where it all got going in a forward direction," Trepanier said. Interestingly, although *PHR* featured the car in September 1987 and again in November 1988, the latter story made no mention of the fact that the car had already been in the magazine once. Perhaps it was because the *PHR* staffer who penned the first article had misspelled the legendary builder's name, listing him as "Troy Trepaier."[2] Respect would soon be earned. *Everyone* in the street machine world would eventually learn how to spell it.

The Chevelle was again lightly updated for the 1989 season with some contemporary Steve Stanford-inspired graphics and a trick new set of Boyd's billet wheels.[5] It had been a well-executed plan Trepanier had discussed with fellow pro street legend Mark Grimes. The idea was to extract the longest possible bit of appeal from the build, keeping it fresh and in the spotlight year after year without having to completely tear it down.[5] But the proverbial wheels were already in motion for Trepanier's next creation, a crossover the likes of which we had never seen.

Soon after the 1989 Nats he sold the Chevelle to his parents and started planning his second car. It wouldn't be pink. It wouldn't be typical. But it would set the hot rodding world on its collective ear. To get outside of the pro street box, Trepanier decided to start *with* a box.

## *Pro Box*

LAUNCH had provided Trepanier with valuable first-hand car crafting experience. It had also helped the young Illinoisan establish himself as a legit up-'n-comer in the street machine world. The classic Chevelle sheet metal wasn't quite risky enough to really make waves, though. All that was about to change in 1989 when Trepanier decided to construct a 1960 Chevy Impala.

"At the time, nobody was doing anything with them—not even restoring them," he later told *Hot Rod*. After sourcing one from an owner in Texas, Trepanier hopped on a plane with a friend and actually drove the low-mileage car all the way home to Manteno.[6,7] With tailfins the size of Howitzer cannons and more glass than a greenhouse, the Impala was on its way to unlikely street machine stardom.

Trepanier promptly got to work, giving the machine the requisite pro street treatment with staggered billet wheels and big-'n-little Mickey Thompson tires. The monochrome look with brushed trim translated well on the Impala's long, sultry body lines, and the unique wintermint green paintjob helped the car further stand out from the pack.

The matching satin-finished and wintermint engine bay sported a tuned port injection system.[6-8] Although commonplace today, such a setup was cutting-edge at the time.

With the growing "Dare to be Different" trend providing all the wind Trepanier's sails could handle, the car was the rage of the '90 Nats, taking Best Engineered, Best Interior, Best Paint, and overall Grand Champion.[8] It landed the cover of *Hot Rod* twice (September and December 1990) and went on to be named the 1990 *Hot Rod* Magazine Hot Rod of the Year.[6,9] At 19, Trepanier was (and remains) the youngest builder in history to win the coveted award.

The car was in intense demand at Du Quoin, where it was photographed for every major custom car magazine. The photo series that appeared in *Car Craft* using the lake and soft grass as a beautiful natural backdrop was a perfect example of the kind of environment Nats showgoers had grown to love. In an interesting bit of Street Machine Nationals trivia, the pictures also just happened to be the work of a serial killer.

Freelance photographer Charles Rathbun was a regular contributor to several major magazines and a frequent presence at Du Quoin in the late '80s and early '90s. Familiar as he was on the grounds, little did anyone know what Rathbun was doing elsewhere in the world. A California jury later convicted Rathbun on multiple counts of sexual assault and murder from 1989-1995—including the high profile case of former Los Angeles Raiders cheerleader Linda Sobek. He was sentenced to life in prison in 1996, but his photos continue to serve as evidence of his time at the Nats, including an encounter with Trepanier's iconic '60 Impala.[10]

In an era dominated by crazy graphics and surging blowers poking through the hood, Pro Box was more akin to a late model street rod than an old pro streeter. The build showed not only Trepanier's creativity but his versatility, as well. After all, it took a 20-year old to show us all how to apply styling cues and tricks the greybeards had used on their '33 Fords and Willys coupes for decades on our own cars. The end result was fantastic.

"I always followed Boyd (Coddington) and was into the street rod thing also, but at the time they didn't cross over much," he said. "Sullivan did it a bit, but he was really the only one. So I decided to do the monochrome, brushed trim, and brushed wheels like Scott (Sullivan) had done and it served as a nice crossover between street rods and street machines," he added.

He was absolutely correct. The car was one of the first to feature Mr. Gasket's "Rodware" line of hardware designed by legendary street rod builder Lil' John Buttera.[6-8]

The Impala was groundbreaking in other ways, too. Trepanier and *Hot Rod* staffer Gray Baskerville drove the car from Indianapolis to Las Vegas for the 1990 SEMA Show, a trek *Hot Rod* chronicled as "The Victory Tour." Along with Scott Sullivan, Bob Maynard, and a bevy of other popular builders, Trepanier and *HR* staffers travelled west from Indy to Vegas in a caravan of custom cars.[11] Along with Jeff Smith's "Pro Interstate" stories with Sullivan, the idea would eventually spawn the Hot Rod Power Tour.

Trepanier even whipped together a pair of motorcycle-style inner fenders to protect his engine compartment on the trip. The move surely saved Pro Box from the asphalt rash sure to come from the four day, 1,800+ mile journey. Like Sullivan before him, Trepanier was convinced that building a show-worthy vehicle wasn't important if it couldn't also be roadworthy, too.

### Bumongous and Beyond

With two feature-quality builds and a den full of awards under his belt before he was even old enough to legally buy a beer, Trepanier changed the game again in 1992 with yet another alternative body style. This time, a monstrous 1950 Buick would serve as the starting point.

"About six miles from the shop is a junkyard, and for about a year and a half I drove by this 1950 Buick sitting in the weeds," he said.[12] Intrigued by the behemoth, bulging body and the distinctive toothed grille, Trepanier again tapped artist Steve Stanford—who had helped previously with the '66 Chevelle—to come up with a concept sketch.[13,14] After deciding to build the car, Trepanier tracked down a suitable starting point in California.

A fuel injected big block and a unique root beer, peach, and orange paint job headlined the build.[15-17] Legendary artist and fellow pro street hero Scott Sullivan was tapped to lay down the trick airbrushed emblems and artwork. The car took a host of awards in Du Quoin in '92, including Best Paint & Graphics, Best Engineered, Best Interior, best Engine, and Pro Show Class Champion.[18] It was named Hot Rod of the Year for 1992, and *Car Craft* named the unique cruiser to its list of Top Ten Street Machines of all time.[19,20] Leveraging his growing brand, Trepanier worked a deal with Orion Car Stereo for a series of promotional spots and "Bumongous" hit celebrity status.

### From Four Rad Rides for Troy to Rad Rides By Troy

Whether it was intentional or not, Trepanier had successfully used the pages of *Hot Rod* and *Car Craft* to establish himself as a recognized name in the street machining world. By the time his fourth creation—a cool little pro street '60 Rambler American wagon—hit the streets, call for his services were mounting. He answered the call and Rad Rides was born.

In characteristic "Troy-Boy" style, the Rambler incorporated a number of street rod influences along with the still popular but soon fading fat-tire look. By the time "Ramblur" hit the magazines in late 1994, pro street was still strong, representing 67% of all *Car Craft*'s features and 51% of *Hot Rod*'s. That would quickly change, though, with only 1996 *Popular Hot Rodding* ever again eclipsing 50% or more pro street coverage.

Unfortunately, by 1994 all editorial coverage for the Street Machine Nationals had left, headed west to *Car Craft*'s newly formed "Summer Cruise." Couple that with the fact that Family Events suffered a loss of files in an office move and a full list of winners of that '94 event no longer exists. What can be confirmed is that the car was on grounds for the first-ever Hot Rod Power Festival, making the September '94 cover of *Hot Rod*.

In predictable Trepanier fashion, the Rambler was named to *Hot Rod*'s Top Ten for 1994, narrowly missing Hot Rod of the Year honors to a questionable 1962 Thunderbird.[21] Although Dare to be Different body styles were hot, it was clear that magazine types were attempting to steer trends away from the 15+ year old pro street look.

Artist Bob Thrash proved to be a valuable asset on the build. Thrash had studied under the tutelage of Scott Sullivan and had given a hand on the Buick. Trepanier entrusted Thrash with the Rambler's graphics and a number of other custom touches. Recalling the Rambler, Trepanier said, "That was the last car I owned."[12]

The next Trepanier-built creation to hit the magazines was a cool pro touring-style 1961 Biscayne built for (and with) his father Jack.[22,23] After a well-executed '39 Chevy coupe was built for Dan Jacobs as the first-ever customer car for the new business, things were looking bright. However, the car that really established Rad Rides as a turn-key builder for the stars was unquestionably George Poteet's '54 Plymouth Savoy—the "Sniper."

With Dodge Viper running gear and Mercedes Benz headlights, the car was decidedly cutting-edge cool and look-at-me different. However, Poteet's deep pockets and excellence-at-any-cost mindset let Trepanier really open his creative stride.

"George Poteet was my first big-time customer—the first guy that said, 'Show me what you can do,'" Trepanier recounted. The revolutionary car scored two full color features in *Hot Rod*: first a build feature in December 1997 and then a completed project feature in February 1998.[24,25]

Trepanier and Poteet would team up for a number of other builds in the future, including a 319 mile-per-hour '69 Barracuda—the "Blowfish"—and a mind-bending '69 Torino. The Torino was so incredible that it landed a 13-page full color feature in *Hot Rod* before it had even been *painted*.[26]

## Hometown Showoff

Du Quoin is a four and a half hour drive from Manteno. However, for a guy used to packing up and heading to SEMA, or the Ridler, or any other national-stage event, the Street Machine Nationals were as close to a backyard gathering as Trepanier would ever get. Location aside, the show still commands a special place in his heart.

"Being in Du Quoin—the premiere event—and making lifelong friends was definitely key for me. Guys like Bret Voelkel, Chic Henry from Australia, all the vendors—those were all contacts I first made in Du Quoin," he admitted. It wasn't all business, though.

"The event was a lot of cruising and just a lot of fun—trying to make a scene and park in the right place. I had a lot of success there, winning five Grand Champion rings, but I'll tell you, the Saturday night parking lots in Marion and Carbondale was some of the most fun I've ever had," Trepanier said with a laugh. "Whether it was setting off fire alarms or completely blowing tires off doing burnouts—when I look at the younger builders at these Goodguys events, I think, 'Wow, this is like tame, baby stuff compared to what we used to do,'" he shared with a chuckle.

Trepanier recalls tons of fun at the event, but scarcely any sleep. "I remember sitting up until 2 in the morning talking and hanging out, drinking Purple Passion, then getting up at like 5 a.m. the next morning to get the car to a photo shoot," he said. "It was the perfect possible place for the event with a ton of great lifelong friends—just a lot of great times down 'ere," he admitted with his distinctive Northern Illinois inflection.

Trepanier is hopeful that a rebirth of the event will take root so that the next generation of car crafters can take inspiration from it just like he did. "Just to go back to that unique venue, and the town—lots of great memories—and even though we've branched out, the core of what we do is street machines."[1]

And for fans of the Street Machine Nationals, Troy Trepanier grew up right before our very eyes: from a simple red '66 Chevelle to a cool '60 Impala, from an Impala to a crazy Buick, and from a Buick to the coolest Rambler wagonever built. Then from a Rambler wagon to one of the most successful shops in the country, we watched it all happen from one year to the next.

That's probably why, even though he's now over 40, Troy Trepanier will forever be "the Kid" to Nats fans.

## References

1. Trepanier T. Custom car builder. Personal communication: Telephone interview. April 10, 2012.
2. Pesterre P. Low Approach. *Popular Hot Rodding*. September 1987:54.
3. Baskerville G. Hot Pink. *Hot Rod*. October 1988:86-87.
4. Hemer C. Out to Launch. *Popular Hot Rodding*. November 1988:56-57.
5. Pitt J. Transportation Transformation. *Car Craft*. April 1990:34-38.
6. Baskerville G. Greenhouse Effect. *Hot Rod*. September 1990:69-76.
7. Hemer C. Troy's Toy. *Popular Hot Rodding*. October 1990:64-65; 110.
8. McGowan J. Grand Slammed. *Car Craft*. November 1990:68-69.
9. Baskerville G. '90 Best of Hot Rod: Top Ten. *Hot Rod*. December 1990:18-21.
10. Krikorkian G, Belgum D. Jury Convicts Rathbun of Model Sobek's Murder. *Los Angeles Times*. November 2, 1996.
11. Baskerville G. On the Road Again. *Hot Rod*. February 1991:60-64.
12. Kinnan R. 25 Years of Troy. *Hot Rod*. June 2013:68-83.
13. Baskerville G. Troy-Boy's New Toy. *Hot Rod*. January 1992:9.
14. Baechtel J. Straight Scoop Garage. *Car Craft*. June 1992:10.
15. Huffman JP. Leviathan. *Car Craft*. August 1992:20-28.
16. Oldham S. 2Big. *Popular Hot Rodding*. December 1992:56-58; 98.
17. Baskerville G. Bumongous. *Hot Rod*. August 1992:58-62.
18. Baechtel J. Show of Force. *Car Craft*. October 1992:18-30.
19. Baskerville G. Top Ten Time. *Hot Rod*. December 1992:54-57.
20. Kiewicz J. Top 10 Street Machines. *Car Craft*. March 1997:26-28.
21. Hardin D. Top Ten. *Hot Rod*. December 1994:56-60.
22. Evans C. BisQuik. *Popular Hot Rodding*. October 1997:22-23.
23. Cook M. Bisquik. *Car Craft*. October 1997:44-46.

24. Baskerville G. Bull's Eye. *Hot Rod*. December 1997:106-110.
25. Baskerville G. Bull's Eye: Part II. *Hot Rod*. February 1998:114-117.
26. Kinnan R. Raw Talent. *Hot Rod*. September 2012:44-57.

# chapter 13

## THE CANUCK
## AL HINDS

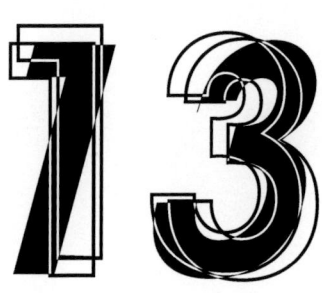

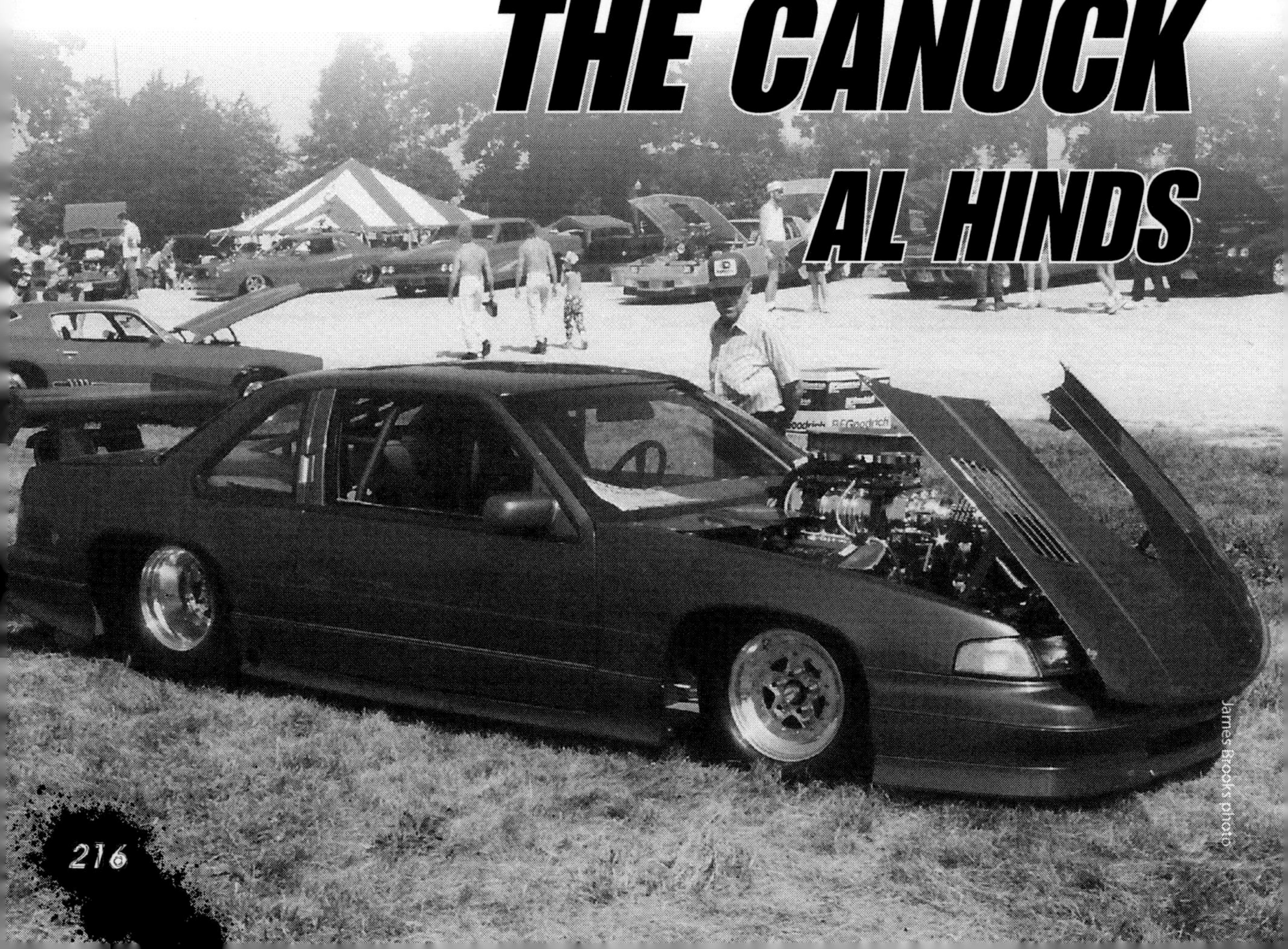

James Brooks photo

chapter 13 | THE CANUCK

## Ice Hockey, Maple Syrup and Mickey Thompsons?

Canada is known for lots of great things. Pristine wilderness? Check. Ice hockey? Check. Maple syrup and Michael J. Fox? Check and check. Those things aside, when considering great cruise spots and epicenters for awesome street machines, it is a sure bet that for most car guys and gals, our neighbors to the north rank pretty far down the list.

Don't blame Al Hinds for that, though.

The likeable Canadian single-handedly put his entire country on the street machining map in the late '80s and early '90s with two consecutive full-bore pro street efforts. He went toe to toe with a number of legendary American pro street builders in the process. He wasn't looking to pick a fight, mind you. He just wanted to build cool cars.

"I was a professional motocross racer until I was 21, and by the time you get to that age in the sport, your career is pretty much over," Hinds recounted.[1] "I sold my last motocross bike and used the money to buy a supercharger for a 1980 Z-28 I was building. I had bought it new when I was 19," he said.[1] The car was Hinds' first foray into going fast on four wheels.

Intrigued by the growing pro street trends he had read about in all the popular car magazines from the States, Hinds decided to make the 800 mile journey south to Du Quoin for the '86 Nats. "I got hooked on it right away," he recalled.

As with so many of his pro street contemporaries, he grew increasingly dissatisfied with his first build. For as nice as the car was, it went largely unnoticed in the sea of tricked out iron on the rolling Southern Illinois countryside.

The tubbed-n-blown second generation Chevy finally landed a shared feature in the February 1989 issue of *Popular Hot Rodding*.[2] But by 1988, Hinds had already made up his mind: he was building a new car.[1] He had decided it was time to go all in.

## *It's a Pro Street World, After All*

By his own admission, Hinds was ready for a place at the big boys' table. He decided to construct a new full-bore Chevy Beretta.

"The Beretta was my first attempt to compete with the Scott Sullivans and the Rocky Robertsons and the Rod Sabourys of the world," he acknowledged. "One of the reasons I got into this was that when I had the Z-28, I was just a guy with a car—a nobody—and I'm still a nobody. But those guys welcomed me like I had been around forever, and that kind of inspired me to try my hand at building something different," he added.

The '89 Beretta was wicked quick and sported clean, modern lines. The car was widely praised for its craftsmanship and performance potential, even though the paint scheme was a bit over the top for some. Even in an era of garish extremes like the late '80s and early '90s, the wild primary greens, blues, reds, and yellows led some to refer to it as "Disney-esqe." Paint criticisms aside, the blown and injected big block was potent, and the car was a far cry from a single-purpose overheating fairgrounds queen.[3,4] It could *go*.

The late-model Chevy body style was smoking hot at the time of the car's debut at Du Quoin in 1990, too. Similar to a number of other late-model builders, Hinds managed to acquire a test car at no cost directly from the automaker to assist in the project.

"I was lucky enough to get some help from General Motors. They donated the car to me. It took a year to get it through all the lawyers and legalities and such, but I finally got it," he said.[1]

Hinds' inspiration for the build came from the Reher-Morrison pro stock car of NHRA driver Bruce Allen. Building a cutting-edge, just-released-to-the-public body style brought with it some challenges, though.

"You had to hurry if you wanted to have the first one," Hinds said. Rich Gebhardt had accomplished that feat with his little orange V-6 car, and a handful of others had debuted in 1989, as well. Not content to simply have one of the first handful of pro streeters with the distinctive new body style, he wanted to be an innovator in other respects, too.

"With that car, I tried to come up with something nobody else had done to make it unique," he said. "That was how I came up with the twin funny car-style 'his-n-hers' rollcages. Lots of guys had a single, so I thought it would be cool to do a double," he added.[1] That same mentality also led to the wild color and graphics choice, too.[3,4]

"The neon colors were just starting to be the rage and I thought that I really wanted it to stand out, so that's what I did. You either hated it or you loved it," he said.

Count *Hot Rod* editor Jeff Smith in the "hated it" category. "He told me it looked like Walt Disney threw up on it," Hinds added.[1] Even super-cool Scott Sullivan graphics on the hood weren't enough to convince the Editor.

As with any bleeding-edge attempt at trendsetting, the risk in such a wild and crazy color palette was big. On the other hand, it was distinctive. *Car Craft* still seemed on the fence about the paintjob in April 1992 when talking about Hinds' new build.

"Al Hinds...psychotically graphic pro street Beretta graced/adorned/dominated/overwhelmed CC's December '90 cover..." it read.[5] Regardless, the Beretta certainly benefitted from excellent magazine exposure, being featured on the cover of the December 1990 *Car Craft* and in a full color spread in the March 1991 *Hot Rod*.[3,4]

Whether that coverage was *because* or *in spite of* the wild paint was open for debate, but nevertheless the car absolutely killed it on the '90 show circuit. At the Street Machine Nationals alone, it had laid claim to first place in Best Graphics and Best use of plating, second place in Best Engine Compartment and best GM, third place in Best Engineered, and Runner Up Grand Champion behind Troy Trepanier's Pro Box '60 Impala.[6]

Hinds had the Beretta on display at the 1990 U.S. Nationals in Indianapolis with a small "for sale" sticker in the window when its eventual new owner would happen by.

"I met Ken and Judy Black in Indy. Before the weekend was over, we struck up a deal and he was going to be the owner of the Beretta," Hinds said.[1]

Shockingly, the legendary drag racer and pro stock owner had become the proud owner of an import car—albeit a blown and injected Beretta from just north of the border. With the Beretta sent packing to Vegas, it was time for Hinds' next effort.

### The Second Movement

"When GM saw the Beretta and how well it turned out in all the magazine coverage that it got, they offered up to do another car," Hinds said. Exhausted from the involved build process of the Beretta, Hinds asked for a year to recuperate and enjoy his efforts at shows across the US before tackling his next project.

"They agreed and I was lucky enough to get the Lumina a year or so later and do the same with it," he said gratefully.

Like the Beretta, the Lumina was heavily influenced by drag racing trends of the time with some subtle and some not-so-subtle Hinds twists. A few build pics managed to find their way into the April 1992 issue of *Car Craft*.[5] The Chevy featured a full tube chassis car with Hinds' signature dual funny car roll cage.[7-9] This time around, the innovative Canadian also opted to add a funny car-style escape hatch in the roof on the driver's side.

## chapter 13 | THE CANUCK

The doghouse of the car was stretched to accommodate the heavy-breathing 572 cubic inch rat perched between the front struts.[7,8]

Also unique for the car was a huge top fuel-style rear wing and an extended single wheel wheelie bar. After countless hours of research and development, Hinds had managed to successfully employ two of Holley's four-barrel replacement Pro-Jection 4 standalone fuel injection units atop the massive 8-71 Littlefield blower.[8] Perhaps most groundbreaking was the rear suspension, influenced heavily by Hinds' years as a motocross racer.

"We came up with this goofy idea of putting a swingarm rear suspension under it, so the shock absorbers were actually mounted in the passenger compartment," he said. "It actually worked. It still had a four-link, but it had this swingarm that nobody else ever did. *Ever*. We took the car to the dragstrip and it actually hooked up really well," he acknowledged.[1]

Determined to sidestep the only real criticisms ever hurled in the direction of the Beretta, Hinds opted to play it safe on the sheetmetal hues this time, selecting a graphics-free straightfoward teal for his new creation.

"I wanted to tone it down a little bit, so that's why I painted it all one color," he said.[1]

Take that, Jeff Smith.

As successful as the Beretta had been, Hinds' second effort had upped the ante. Not only was it featured in all three major magazines, it took the cover of the August 1992 issue of *Car Craft* and the September 1992 issue of *Hot Rod*.[10] It also competed admirably in *Car Craft's* "Pro Street Shootout" and was later named a Hot Rod Top Ten car for 1992.[11,12]

At the Street Machine Nationals, it took Best Engine (only winners in each category were published; those that placed were not).[13] In a tough year to debut a new car against the likes of Troy Trepanier, Chris Embree, Frank Guidace, and Richard Boyd, the Lumina had been yet another success for the affable Canadian.

After the 1992 Nats, *Car Craft* had set up its "Pro Street Shootout," and pro stock racer Buddy Ingersoll showed up in his controversial turbo V-6 Buick to blast a few passes down the eighth-mile strip.

"Without slicks, I smoked the tires the whole length of the track," Hinds recalled. "I'll never forget this—Buddy Ingersoll comes over to me, and with that heavy Southern drawl he says, 'Son, you got way too much horsepower for this here racetrack,'" he said with a chuckle.[1]

With slicks, the car ran a quarter mile equivalent of a 10-second pass (6.50 @ 108.69 in the eighth mile) through the mufflers.[12] Once fully sorted and back in Canada, the 3,500 pound car with real steel body panels and full glass went a best of 9.40 seconds at 140 miles per hour in the quarter mile.[1]

Hinds ultimately sold the Lumina to a buyer in Kentucky. The two hit it off and became fast friends. A while later when the new owner decided he was ready to move the car to finance his growing drag racing habit, Hinds offered to help him sell it.

"We ended up letting it go to a guy in California. A little while later I pick up this street rod magazine with a big centerfold of the Lumina claiming how this shop out in California built it," he said. "You can imagine how I felt, so I called up the magazine and tore them a new one. I was like, 'Have you been living under a rock for two years? This car has been a Hot Rod Top Ten of the Year and in every major magazine already. You've never seen it before?'" he said incredulously.

Ultimately, the car changed hands again, this time landing in Boston. On a tip from a friend, Hinds found the car on eBay in the late '90s. Curious, he contacted the new owner just to see what it might take to get the car back.

"Most car guys are cool. I call this guy up and he's a real prick—until he found out I was the guy who built it—then he was like my best friend," he said with a laugh.

Ultimately Hinds lost track of the car, but he is still interested in reacquiring it should it surface again for a fair price.

### Street Machine Internationals

Hinds said he became a raving ran of the Nats from the moment he set foot on the Du Quoin State Fairgrounds in 1986. "Besides all the cars, the

## chapter 73 | THE CANUCK

best thing was the great people I met," Hinds reflected. "Guys like top alcohol dragster driver Dave Hirata, Rod Saboury, the late Stan Shaw—those were lifelong friends that I met at the show," he added.

Like many, he recalled the nighttime activities in Du Quoin as being most memorable. "My wife Dee and I were in the Beretta one night and I was a little skeptical about taking the car out," he recalled. Partiers in the hotel parking lot convinced Hinds to strike the rear tires on his way off the property.

"These guys are dumping hotel trash cans full of water and telling me to do a burnout. So I did the meanest, nastiest, funny car-style burnout you've ever seen. When I came back later they started yelling and getting all ticked off because they said I had dried up all their water," he added with a hearty laugh.

Hinds recalled the citizens of Du Quoin as gracious hosts who knew how to have a good time. "They were good about letting us come in and terrorize their town," he said. He is also thrilled at the notion of returning for a reunion of sorts. "Although I don't have a pro street car anymore, I can't wait to bring my pro mod car down. I can't wait to go again," he added.

In the years since his moment in the pro street spotlight, Hinds did two things consistently. First, he has kept right on working as a salesman at a Chevy dealership—a trade he has refined over the last 30+ straight years—and he drag raced. Most recently, his quarter mile money pit has been a wild pro mod car. "I miss the building part and the creativity of pro street, but honestly I got into the drag cars because I never really drove my street cars," he said.

When asked for further reflection on the show, Hinds paused momentarily. "You know, I didn't go to the shows to get the awards," he said deliberately. "I went to the shows for the magazine coverage."

In fact, Hinds said he recently had to clean out several boxes of awards that he had collected over the years that hadn't even been opened, opting to donate them to a local car club. While he chose to hang onto a few that held particular sentimental value, he repurposed those that were simply taking up space.

It was, in Hinds' estimation, the editorial coverage that was critical to the success of both the car and the builder. "Because I had some help from several manufacturers with parts and products, I wanted to get them some exposure for their participation. So the magazine coverage was crucial for me—that and just the fun of going to the events," he said. "If I wouldn't have won one trophy, I wouldn't have cared. As long as I got in the magazines, I was a happy guy," he added.

Hinds is quick to credit his beloved wife of 26 years, Dee. "I could never have done any of this without her support," he said. "Still to this day she tries to one-up my cars with her collection of shoes," he added.

Considering none of Dee's shoes have been featured in a magazine yet, I'd say Al still holds a slight advantage.

Only Hinds knows for certain whether he has built his last pro street car, but one thing is for sure: Du Quoin was a far cry from his hometown of Waterloo, Ontario, in more ways than one.

One year at the Nats, Hinds' car had puked a radiator hose and he had it up on jackstands to clean off the mess and repair the damage. He had walked into the Mr. Gasket trailer that had been set up as a mobile garage for just such an occurrence to get some tools. Before he could exit, a topless young lady approached and matter-of-factly told him how much she loved his car. She then merrily headed on her way. No big deal, right?

"That kinda crap don't jus' happen everyday in Waterloo!" he said. A crazy situation for some, it was business as usual at the Nats.

Lucky for the bare-chested showgoer Dee wasn't around at the time. Chances are good there would have been a good ol' fashioned Canadian-style designer-shoe-wearing butt kicking to follow.

## *References*

1. Hinds A. Custom car builder. Personal communication: Telephone interview. April 12, 2012.
2. Reyes S. Camaros: A Collage of Ground-Pounding, Tire-Frying, Bow-Tie Beauties. Popular Hot Rodding. February 1989:28.
3. McGowan J. Beretta, eh? Car Craft. December 1990:58-59.
4. Anderson S. Hindsight. Hot Rod. March 1991:100-101.
5. Baechtel J. Straight Scoop Garage. Car Craft. April 1992:10.
6. Rathbun C. Street Machine Nats '90. Car Craft. October 1990:18-43.
7. Smith J. Zoomina! Hot Rod. October 1992:40-41.
8. Huffman JP. Northern Exposure. Car Craft. August 1992:34-40.
9. Fetherston D. Green Light. Popular Hot Rodding. November 1992:56.
10. Pettitt J. Power on Parade. Hot Rod. September 1992:30-40.
11. Baskerville G. Top Ten Time. Hot Rod. December 1992:54-57.
12. Baechtel J. Pro Street Shootout. Car Craft. November 1992:18-28.
13. Baechtel J. Show of Force. Car Craft. October 1992:18-30.

# chapter 14

# MR. NATIONALS
## BRET VOELKEL

chapter 14 | MR. NATIONALS

## *The Whim that Changed Hot Rodding*

**W**hat do you call a guy who has attended nearly every Street Machine Nationals ever either as a spectator, a vendor, or a participant? Who built the first-ever air ride suspension equipped pro street car? Who founded a first-of-its-kind business that has grown into a multi-million dollar enterprise in just over a decade? Who currently dominates autocross events across the country in a 2,600 pound, 440-horsepower dart of a '33 Ford? Who has landed a feature car in a major national automotive magazine in each of the past three decades, including the cover of *Hot Rod* as recently as July 2013?

Simple. Call him Bret.

Bret Voelkel grew up a typical Midwest kid in Jasper, Indiana. However, unlike many of his hot rodding contemporaries, he didn't come from a long line of gearheads. And although his high school buddies like Greg Schneider, Scott Mehringer, and a few others were into cars just like he was, none of them came from bona fide street machining roots, either.

"The unusual thing is that none of our families were involved in hot rodding, racing, or any of that kind of stuff," Voelkel said.[1] In their teen years, Voelkel and his gang's burgeoning love for working on cars likely came from necessity.

"In high school when we all started driving, we quickly figured out that we had to fix our own stuff or walk, and that's kind of how it came about," he acknowledged.

Voelkel first attended the Street Machine Nationals as an impressionable young local at the third annual event in Indy in 1979. After learning about the show from a radio ad, he and a friend—bored and looking for something to do—decided on a whim to check it out. A quick trip some 130 miles northeast to the Indianapolis State Fairgrounds and Voelkel would be changed for life.

## *The Civilian Years and Beyond*

The sight of 3,000 or more street machines and the countless throng of onlookers was simply incredible. After attending his first event in '79, Voelkel was hooked.

"I always call that show 'Christmas in June,'" he said.

So powerful was the pull of the Nats that the young Hoosier actually quit two or three jobs simply because supervisors had refused to give him the weekend of the show off. "I'd ask off and these places would say, 'No, you can't have off.' So I'd say, 'Well, that's fine. I quit,'" he said with a chuckle.[1]

Inspired by the craftsmanship he saw at the show, in 1984, Voelkel's own 1970 fastback Mustang was featured in *Popular Hot Rodding*.[2] After being heavily influenced by the trends and tricks he had seen as a Street Machine Nationals regular, Voelkel built the car from the ground up.

The car was a basket case when he acquired it in 1980, but Voelkel had managed to convert it into a smooth and stylish cruiser with a potent 429, iconic Cragar SST wheels, a snorkel scoop, and a clean yellow paint job with blacked out chrome trim. The often-copied orange and yellow graphics were applied by fellow Street Machine Nationals legends Bob and Danny Taylor of Taylor's House of Colors in Louisville, Kentucky.[2]

The car later appeared on the cover of *Car Craft* in their event coverage of the 1985 Street Machine Nationals.[3] By that time, Voelkel had ditched the snorkel scoop and 429 in favor of a 460 with a tunnel ram with dual Predators, and the Cragars had been replaced with Weld Draglites.

It was a solid effort for a 22-year old who had been completely self-taught in the street machining scene. However, it was just the tip of the iceberg for the wild, groundbreaking creations in Voelkel's future.

As Voelkel tells it, after his first experience in 1979, he attended the next seven events as a "civilian." However, by 1987—the show's second year in Du Quoin—he had made street machines his vocation. As a result, he worked the '87 event as a sales representative for the first time.

## *Workin' It*

"I got a job as a tech rep at the drag races for a company that represented a number of aftermarket manufacturers—Auto Meter, MSD, Edelbrock, B&M, and places like that," he said. As a result, his employer, World of Performance in Orlando, Florida, assigned him to the show as an Auto Meter rep. He did the same in 1988 and 1989.

"I remember in 1988, it was 109 degrees that weekend," he said. "It was so hot that when people walked across the asphalt, the tar bubbled up and it would stick to their shoes," he said. Such conditions didn't exactly make for an ideal work environment. However, Voelkel says he wouldn't have preferred to be anywhere else on the planet.

"It was miserable, but the bright side was that the females tended to be pretty scantily clothed, so most guys didn't complain too much," he added with a laugh.

Never one to fail to help his fellow man (or in this case woman), Voelkel recognized the need for relief from the stifling heat. The Auto Meter trailer had been positioned near a water hydrant, so the resourceful young rep went and bought a water hose and nozzle in order to set up an impromptu "misting" station. Although detractors could have referred to the setup as a "wet t-shirt" station, as with many things at Du Quoin, it was all a matter of one's perspective.

"Doug Evans—who is now Executive VP at Source Interlink, but at the time was Director of Operations of that show—came by and raised a little fuss at me for doing that," Voelkel recalled. "But not until after he sat there on his golf cart and watched it all happen for about 45 minutes," he added with a chuckle. Such was life at the Street Machine Nationals.

Voelkel transitioned to a position as Mobile Motorsports Director with Blower Drive Service (BDS) in 1990. The man who had previously quit multiple jobs as a youth so that he could attend the Street Machine Nationals was now on his second position that actually *required* attendance at the show.

"BDS was one of the big sponsors of the event at that time, so we had a prime parking spot on the corner of the Manufacturer's Midway," he recalled. That first year with the company, Voelkel and BDS Marketing Director Larry Hall managed to sell more than 600 t-shirts on the weekend, each emblazoned with the now-infamous "Injection is Nice, But I'd Rather Be Blown" logo. Now owner of an incredibly successful business of his own since 1996, Voelkel says he probably hasn't sold that many t-shirts *total* in the two and a half decades since the event.

Far from a work-only assignment, Voelkel fondly remembers what he refers to as the "night scene" at the Street Machine Nationals. More often than not, Saturday nights involved hours of hanging out in motel parking lots watching spontaneous burnout contests. And in Voelkel's case, participating in them, as well.

"I met Troy Trepanier for the first time in 1988 when he was 16 and I was 26 and he had his pink '66 Chevelle," Voelkel said. "I had a '79 Ford Fairmont at the time with a blower and 2.73 rearend in it—so it would smoke the tires until you got bored with it. So I did about a three-minute burnout and filled the whole parking lot with smoke," he added.

Not to be outdone, the competitive teen and future Rad Rides founder hopped in his tow vehicle—a '73 Buick Riviera—and proceeded to roast his rear tires so furiously that he actually set off the fire alarms inside the motel. After a brief visit from the local fire department, order was restored.

"By the time we were done, my tires were pretty bald. I had to buy new tires for my car once I got home," Voelkel said.

Trepanier would not be so lucky.

"Troy, on the other hand, had to buy new tires to *get* home—he had to go to Benton or somewhere to actually buy a used set of tires for that Buick just to make it back to Manteno," he said with a laugh.

Times were not always just good old-fashioned fun at the Nats night scene. In Indianapolis, Voelkel can recall police turning dogs loose to disperse a rowdy crowd on 21st and Shadeland Avenue. A similar gathering a few years later in Springfield resulted in authorities employing fire hoses to break up a gathering on Dirksen & Stephenson Drive. He also recalls the incredible police presence in Du Quoin, as well. "I'm told they had the biggest collection of Illinois State Troopers since they filmed the *Blues Brothers*," he stated.[1]

Voelkel's experiences lodging for the weekend are likely familiar to many showgoers from the time. "We would go over there—usually about a dozen of us—we would buy fuel for the cars, then we'd buy beer, then we'd buy cigarettes, then with whatever money we had left over, we bought rooms," he said. "So we ended up with two—sometimes three—rooms for a dozen people. Guys, girls, it didn't matter. It was all just one big happy family," he added.

## Built Not Bought

Voelkel's next ride that garnered magazine exposure was a tasteful monochromed '79 Ford Fairmont that was shot for *Car Craft* at the '91 Nats.[4] The car was tastefully executed, but what really set it apart from the crowd was its electronic fuel injection system perched atop a BDS blower. A rep for BDS at the time, Voelkel used the car as a rolling billboard of sorts for the supercharger supply house.

By far the most famous car Voelkel ever brought to the Nationals was also the one that ignited a revolution in hot rodding and helped him kick off his business enterprise, Air RideTechnologies (now RideTech) in 1996.

"My first air suspension car—the orange and white blown and injected pro street Mustang—was probably the most popular one I ever took there," he said.

The car would go on to earn Best Ford at the '96 Nationals as well as a number of other pro street honors.[5] It also landed a cover spot on the October '96 *Popular Hot Rodding* as well as full color features in both *Popular Hot Rodding* and *Hot Rod*.[5-7]

Sadly and inexplicably, for the first time in decades, *Hot Rod* failed to publish its wildly popular Top Ten list for 1997 (the year the car appeared in the magazine), but it is safe to say that if then-Editor Ro McGonegal and his colleagues had created such a list, the game-changing Mustang should have been on it.

Although air suspensions had started making their way into the mini-truck and sport truck worlds at the time, until Voelkel did it on the 'Stang, they really hadn't been employed on hot rods or street machines to any significant extent. Voelkel and his crew from Jasper were about to change all that forever. The combination of slammed show stance and smooth street ride made it a natural fit. Air RideTechnologies—and later RideTech—was born.[8]

The Mustang was far from a one-trick pony, though. In addition to the groundbreaking adjustable ride-height suspension, the car featured a wicked-looking satin finished 8-71 BDS blower with a 16-nozzle electronic fuel injection system and an old-school brushed injector hat. A factory-appearing—but never available—hatchback body headlined a long list of body mods. The entire effort was topped off by some subtle but intricate Bob Maynard graphics that took over 70 hours to lay down.[6]

Maynard was no slouch himself. His 1971 pale blue Camaro had been a surprise hit of the 1990 Nats. The dare-to-be-different second-gen was "motorvated" by a pink inline 6-cylinder with nitrous and the car was picked up for *Hot Rod* and *Car Craft* shortly after the Du Quoin event.[9-11] Voelkel had been so impressed with the understated but highly detailed graphics on Maynard's Camaro that he knew he wanted him to shoot the Mustang.

Voelkel's steed also featured en vogue creature comforts like air conditioning and the cutting-edge EFI system meant the 700 horsepower 351 Windsor still managed a respectable 15 mpg on the highway. Pro street had indeed come a long way, and the "Super 'Stang" had helped show the rest of the world that fairgrounds cool didn't have to mean a car had to be towed around everywhere it went.[7]

## *It's Been a Wild Ride(tech)*

From those early beginnings, RideTech has grown to become the number one source for street machine and hot rod air suspension components in the world. The company has also expanded to include a full line of high quality, state-of-the-art traditional suspension products such as control arms, four-links, and coil overs, too. Toss in other items like stainless roll cages and military applications, and it is a thriving, made-in-America success story of a bright entrepreneur who has literally built his business the same way he built his first magazine-quality car: from the ground up. Voelkel wouldn't have it any other way.

"RideTech keeps me and about 38 others going pretty good," he said. Most recently, the company completed a supercar-killing '33 Factory Five hot rod that Voelkel has piloted at autocross events around the country.[12] The car was originally built as a rolling test bed for RideTech components, but Voelkel is unapologetic in admitting that the car has been an absolute thrill to drive. A photo of Voelkel piloting the '33 while leaving a hapless Lamborghini in his wake commanded the cover of the July 2013 *Hot Rod*.[12]

"Originally, the intention was to build something light, throw something together, and go fast," he said. Furthermore, as Voelkel tells it, "RideTech uses 'suspension research and development' as a great excuse to build hot rods."[13] Whatever the reason, the end result was a handcrafted, flat black, tire-scalding, pavement gripping ride-on-rails that ultimately captured the 2012 Goodguys overall pro class and street rod class championships.[13]

It is no exaggeration to say that the spark that lit the fuse for the prolific hot rod builder and businessman was a chance encounter at a phenomenon of a car show, the Nats, that he first stumbled across in 1979.

Voelkel says without hesitation that the show has always been the highlight of his year. "I go to a bunch of shows—probably 25 or 30 a year—but I still remember the Street Machine Nationals as being the favorite one," he said. Participants and spectators alike can expect to see Voelkel and RideTech in full force for the 2013 Street Machine Nationals reunion show and beyond.

And who knows, times have sure changed. Voelkel may even have room in the RideTech display trailer for an extra set of tires or two. They may come in handy should his friend from Rad Rides find himself in need just to get back to Manteno again.

## References

1. Voelkel B. RideTech Founder. Personal communication: Telephone interview. April 17, 2012.
2. Benty C. Mellow Yellow. *Popular Hot Rodding*. November 1984:80-81.
3. Boales K. Street Machine Nationals. *Car Craft*. October 1985:18-26.
4. Martin I. Far-Out Fairmont. *Car Craft*. November 1991:82-83.
5. Evans C. Central Park. For Street Machines, That Is. *Popular Hot Rodding*. October 1996:70-73.
6. McClurg B. Hoosier Hauler. *Popular Hot Rodding*. November 1996:22-23.
7. Handzel W. Super 'Stang. *Hot Rod*. January 1997:80-81.
8. RideTech. About Us. 2013; http://www.ridetech.com/info/about/. Accessed March 21.
9. Kinnan R. Out of the Blue. *Hot Rod*. November 1990:66-67.
10. Martin I. Pro Street Sixation. *Car Craft*. May 1991:86-87.
11. Maynard B. Custom car builder. Personal communication: Telephone interview. April 12, 2012.
12. Scherr E. No Bull: RideTech's Bret Voelkel built a Supercar-Shaming '33 Hot Rod, and We Tested It. *Hot Rod*. July 2013:36-44.
13. RideTech. 33 Ford: Year in Review. 2012; http://www.ridetech.com/33ford/. Accessed March 12, 2012.

# chapter 15

# DON'T GO AWAY MAD (JUST GO AWAY) 1994-1998

## chapter 15 | DON'T GO AWAY MAD (JUST GO AWAY)

*Seasons must change*
*Separate paths, separate ways*
*If we blame it on anything*
*Let's blame it on the rain*
*I knew it all along*
*I'd have to write this song*
*Too young to fall in love*
*Guess we knew it all along*

*Held our dreams in our hands*
*Let our minds run away*
*That's alright, now that's okay*
*We were walkin' through some youth*
*Smilin' through some pain*
*That's alright, let's turn the page*
*And remember what I say girl*
*And it goes this way*

*Girl, don't go away mad*
*Girl, just go away*

"Don't Go Away Mad (Just Go Away)," by Nikki Sixx; © copyright 1989, Downtown Music Publishing International, Inc., WB Music Corp[1]

### You're Either Growin' or You're Dyin'

The February 1994 issue of *Car Craft* looked pretty much like any other. There were features of cool cars, tech articles, and all the usual recurring columns. Heck, Gary Buckles' incredible pro street '71 Camaro had even helped make the cover cooler than usual. However, tucked away inconspicuously on page nine was a prophetic obituary of sorts.[2]

The Street Machine Nationals were being strangled.

Within four years, they would be dead.

It wasn't just the Nats, mind you. Pretty much all the events Hubley had purchased from Petersen Publishing in 1986 were being replicated by the former partner and publication giant in 1994. The Car Craft Summer Cruise of Petersen countered the Street Machine Nationals of Family Events. Likewise, the Supernationals were up against the Hot Rod Power Festival. The Offroad Jamboree was up against the 4-Wheel & Off-Road 4 X Fun Fest.

The hyperbole in the pages of the magazines was almost too much to swallow. "*Car Craft* started the event craze during the mid-Seventies with the wild, and sometimes controversial, Car Craft Street Machine Nationals. If you want your car in *Car Craft* during 1994, you need to be at the Car Craft Magazine Summer Cruise," *CC* Editor Chuck Schifsky wrote. He also referred to the Summer Cruise by explicitly calling it "What we think will be the greatest street machine event ever."[2]

The October 1994 issue featured a familiar cover shot with one exception. Ever since 1977, the October cover of *Car Craft* had included photos or—at the very least, a *mention*—of the Street Machine Nationals. Although the magazine's face looked just the same, the text had subtly changed. Out was the Street Machine Nationals. In was the Summer Cruise, heralded as the "Hottest Event of '94."

The thing was, it wasn't. It wasn't even close. The Nats drew a new all-time Du Quoin record of 3,709 cars and a respectable 103,468 spectators. Meanwhile, the Summer Cruise in Sedalia drew less than 500 cars and 10,000 spectators.[3] An unsuspecting reader never would have known it, though.

*Car Craft* made no mention of the turnout in their editorial coverage but did manage to poke a few thinly veiled insults at the Nats, telling readers to "forget about those other wimpy car shows you've heard about" and insisting "...the Car Craft Summer Cruise is the real thing."[4] Photos had been expertly staged to make the fairgrounds appear to be busting at the seams with cars and showgoers. The reality proved far different.

## chapter 15 | DON'T GO AWAY MAD (JUST GO AWAY)

Meanwhile, Du Quoin kept right on going. Sadly, with magazine coverage now locked exclusively on Petersen events per Dianna's mandate from on high, the perception of the show in the minds of many would soon change. Gone were the glory days in which big-time builders thrashed for weeks on end just to get their creations done in time for the big reveal at Du Quoin.

Magazine coverage or not, the show was still impressive.

Gary Buckles' '71 Camaro—debuted earlier in the summer at the Hot Rod Power Fest and the Car Craft Summer Cruise—was on display. So too was Rocky Robertson's flamed and double-blown '51 Kaiser. Dave VerSchave's '66 Nova took the Pro Engineered class champion title and familiar names like Richard Boyd and his '85 Camaro attended, as well.[5]

The hometown newspaper seemed to push hard in their efforts to paint the show in the worst possible light. Although the page header of the *Evening Call*'s coverage of the event claimed "'94 Street Machine Nationals See Milder Crowd," the next line (in larger font) referred to the show as a "Beer 'n Breast Fest."[6]

Other damning evidence mounted, too.

"The Street Machine Nationals had a negative effect on business for many area merchants," reported *Call* writer Annette Holder.[7] However, beneath the headline, those who claimed to have missed out on business over the weekend indicated that it wasn't a big deal, giving them time they wouldn't have otherwise had to perform inventory. Meanwhile, other business owners reported as much as a 400% increase in sales as a result of the show. Apparently that data wasn't compelling enough to find its way into the big typeface.

### *Stayin' Alive*

The show returned to Du Quoin for 1995 and—just like the year before—no magazines covered the event. In town for their 10th straight show in '95, the Nats were in the final year of a five-year agreement with the State of Illinois.[8] Participation was again excellent, with 3,712 registered cars and 106,953 spectators.[9]

Illinois State Police characterized the crowd as calmer than usual. "It's one of the better years," said ISP master sergeant Carletos Meeks.[10] With the projected $15-$16.5 million impact of the show and the State Police's contention that the event was improving, it appeared to be maintaining its position as the premiere street machine gathering in the nation.[9,11]

Familiar faces still mingled through the crowd. Rick Dobbertin showed up in Du Quoin in his milk-tanker-turned-amphibious-vehicle, the Dobbertin Surface Orbiter. Rocky Robertson had helped friend Billy Wooten lay down a cool bubbled three-color graphics job on his '65 Chevelle. Buckles was back again, taking the Pro Engineered Best Engineered title.[11]

Meanwhile in Sedalia, Missouri, at the Summer Cruise, the sibling rivalry continued to fester. *Car Craft* and *Hot Rod* continued to cover the event, with *Hot Rod* spilling the beans that the show had mustered only a paltry 600 cars and 9,000 spectators.[12]

*CC* claimed the show had "blown Sedaliaites out of their rocking chairs."[13] If that were the case, imagine what would have happened if the Nats had come to town.

The 1996 Nats proved to be the best attended installment of the show ever, with nearly 110,000 spectators coming to partake of the action.[14] Car count was up from the year before, too, with a record-tying 3,781 cars (equal to turnout in 1993) prowling the fairgrounds in Du Quoin.[14] Non-Petersen Publication title *Popular Hot Rodding* provided event coverage for the show for the first time ever, devoting five pages to Nats happenings in their October '96 issue.[14]

In now-familiar fashion, state police claimed the '96 event was "quieter than a year ago," and that crowds in popular congregating spots mostly broke up before midnight.[15] Both tickets and arrests were lower than normal but still topped 100 by weekend's end.[16]

On the fairgrounds, local Terry Podschweit and son Rodney from nearby West Frankfort captured Grand Champion Street Machine, Best Paint, Best Graphics, Best Ford, Best Ford Pro Street, and Best Engine Compartment.[17] Fellow West Frankforter George Norovich also took home a box full of trophies with his '55 Chevy 210.[18]

## chapter 15 | DON'T GO AWAY MAD (JUST GO AWAY)

Few recognized it at the time, but the lack of geographic diversity of the winners was actually a sign of trouble. The event was becoming less and less the Street Machine "Nationals" and more and more the Street Machine "Regionals."

That sentiment would be shared by at least one unhappy attendee. Show goer Tom Shatner from Burke, Virginia, was so disgusted at the event that he wrote a letter to the editor of *PHR* that appeared in the December '96 issue. After driving 14 hours, Shatner and his friends were underwhelmed.

"I don't mean to take anything away from the quality of the cars, but they were definitely few and far between. The vast majority of the show consisted of lowered mini-trucks with undersized tires and boom boxes," he wrote disgustedly. Although Shatner's group had originally intended to stay for the entire weekend, "…after about four hours we decided to cut our losses and head for home," he concluded.[19]

In their response to Shatner's letter, *PHR* echoed these growing concerns. "The Du Quoin event had the variety we expected, but we did notice license plates mostly from Illinois, Michigan, Kentucky, and Tennessee."[19]

Without question, three of the coolest cars on the grounds in '96 were Bret Voelkel's air ride-equipped pro street '70 Mustang, Steve Gantz's cammer-equipped arrest-me red '65 Corvette, and Kim Gough's radical '74 Laguna. Voelkel's ride was innovative and well-executed. Gantz's Corvette was absolutely stunning. Gough and his incredible blown, injected, and nitroused 427 Chevy was wicked and nasty. All three just missed the Grand Champion title.

Opposition to the show was nothing new, but area resident Bruce Summers had heard enough both around town and in the pages of the hometown *Call*. His Letter to the Editor had some valid points. Recurrent complaints of the excess trash problem were never met with any attempts to increase trashcans around town. Perhaps most importantly, Summers pointed out that the residents of ten homes on Washington Street near the fairgrounds—portrayed in several media outlets, including the *Call,* as "prisoners in their own homes" all weekend once a year—actually regularly sat in their yards in lawn chairs to watch the show.[20]

His points apparently fell on deaf ears, as no one offered any response to his suggestions.

The Street Machine Nationals reached legal age in 1997, as the 21st installment of the show came back to Du Quoin for the 12th straight time on June 27. Both participant and spectator count dipped compared to '96, but a total of 3,709 cars and 105,623 spectators still passed through the fairground gates.[21]

Johnny Young's cool '60 Ford Starliner was the hit of the show. The car sported a wild orange and maroon paint scheme and a potent shotgun scoop topped, fuel injected, and nitroused powerplant to turn the fat rear tires. A number of other familiar pro street cars were in attendance, as well.[21]

Although still popular on the fairgrounds, pro street had really fallen on hard times in the magazines. Long gone were the days when over half of all feature cars sported wheel tubs and a narrowed rear end. Although 41% of *Popular Hot Rodding*'s features in '96 were of the pro street variety, *Car Craft* and *Hot Rod* weighed in at only 24% and 22% respectively. Pro touring had surpassed pro street in the minds of many.

The 1997 Miss Street Machine Nationals, Raina Lenzi hailed from nearby Carbondale. "It was a lot of fun. Everyone was very respectful and well behaved, as far as I was concerned," she said.[22] In addition to claiming the title in '97, Lenzi was named First Runner-Up in '98.[23]

Big changes were announced for the show for 1998. Most importantly, the pre-'49 model year restriction that had originally made the show so unique had been lifted. The event also moved from its familiar spot the last weekend in June to June 12-14 to avoid a conflict with the nearby NHRA race in Joliet.[24] The moves wouldn't be enough to curb the slide in participation. The show drew fewer than 3,500 cars and 100,000 spectators for the first time in a decade.

*Popular Hot Rodding*'s coverage of the event conveyed the sentiment everyone else was thinking: It just wasn't the same. "Many of the cars in the pro-built area were ones we'd seen before, and those that were debuts didn't exhibit any one characteristic that we thought would drive an industry," wrote *PHR* staffer Cameron Evans.[23] By the time the article went to press,

Special Events and officials in Du Quoin had already publically announced their decision to part ways.

It had been a wild and oftentimes contentious 13 years. There had unquestionably been resistance to the show during its entire tenure in Du Quoin. In the end, as *PHR*'s Evans accurately summed up: "The residents of Du Quoin decided they liked a convenient trip to the market more than thousands of dollars of tax revenue."[25]

The student-run Southern Illinois University newspaper—*The Daily Egyptian*— was the only local news outlet that bothered to say anything other than good riddance to the show. In a non-attributed opinion piece lamenting the loss of the event, a columnist wrote, "Another phase of American strength has been vanquished. The stuffy politicians in Illinois are now reveling in delight."[26]

It was over.

Or so we thought.

## Life After the Dooky

The 1999 installment of the Nats landed upstate in Joliet at freshly-opened Route 66 Dragway. By Nats' standards, it was a disappointing turnout of just under 2,500 cars and 50,000 spectators.[25] *PHR* hinted that there had been issues, stating "…the event had its share of first-year 'teething' problems." Their coverage also indicated that Special Events would be one and done at the venue.

Meanwhile, the *Chicago Tribune* came right out and said it: Joliet police and officials didn't want it back. Ever. The city's Chief of Police, Dave Gerdes, was short and to the point with the *Tribune* staffer.

"Hopefully it will be a one-time event for Joliet. It was thrown out of Du Quoin because of all the problems they had down there with spectators and it should be canceled here, too," he said.[27]

After a one-year hiatus in 2000, Family Events resurrected the show for 2001. Opting to host it in their own backyard and return the event to its

roots, the Nats were again held at the Indianapolis State Fairgrounds for the first time since 1981.

It didn't help. With just 1,682 cars and 32,000 spectators, it was—by all estimates—a horrible disappointment. Even though promoters tried to play up the "25th Anniversary" aspect of the show, it seemed to have little impact. After another lackluster iteration in 2002, the show was sentenced to its final stop: Lima, Ohio.

The relationship between Family Events and Peterson Publishing had been understandably icy ever since Dianna and company opted to get back into the show promotion business in 1994. However, things changed pretty abruptly after the often-controversial and widely disliked Peterson VP stepped down in January, 2000.

Promotion, marketing, and delivery of all the Peterson Publication—now PRIMEDIA—automotive events, including the Car Craft Summer Cruise and the Hot Rod Power Tour, were reassigned. In an odd twist, Hubley and his charges were now responsible for both their own events *and* those that had been created and so aggressively marketed against them by Dianna and company just a few years earlier.[28-31] Family Events still manages each of those events today.

It's unlikely you'd be able to find anyone who attended the Street Machine Nationals in its heyday who was also present for the last two versions of the show in Lima in 2003 and 2004. Heck, it's probably hard enough to find anyone who attended the two shows in Lima *at all*. Participation data for the 2003 show was never published. The final year of the show in 2004, only 791 cars and just under 15,000 participants bothered to make the journey to the Allen County Fairgrounds.[32] It was an emaciated, withered, dying shell of its former grandeur.

Family Events did the honorable thing in 2005. They pulled the plug on the oft-maligned show. As *The Daily Egyptian* claimed six years prior, the age of American machismo was dead.[26]

Or was it?

## chapter 15 | DON'T GO AWAY MAD (JUST GO AWAY)

*References*

1. eLyrics.com. Don't Go Away Mad (Just Go Away) lyrics. http://www.elyrics.net/read/m/motley-crue-lyrics/don_t-go-away-mad-lyrics.html, March 17, 2013.
2. Schifsky C. Car Craft Summer Cruise. *Car Craft*. February 1994:9.
3. Hardin D. Summer Cruise: Car Craft Goes Back to its Roots. *Hot Rod*. November 1994:86-87.
4. Schifsky C. In This Issue. *Car Craft*. October 1994:5.
5. Croessman J. Frank, Martha Morgenstern of Du Quoin Win Best Car Paint/Graphics. *Du Quoin Evening Call*. June 27, 1994.
6. Croessman J. '94 Street Machine Nationals See Milder Crowd. *Du Quoin Evening Call*. June 25, 1994.
7. Holder A. Du Quoin Business Owners: Profits Down for Many When Street Machines In Town. *Du Quoin Evening Call*. June 28, 1994.
8. Croessman J. NATs Exhibitors Roll Into Du Quoin; One Year Left on 5-Year Contract. *Du Quoin Evening Call*. June 21, 1995.
9. Croessman J. 1956 Ford Grand Champion at the Street NATs. *Du Quoin Evening Call*. June 26, 1995.
10. Holder A. Street Machine Nationals Weekend at a Glance. *Du Quoin Evening Call*. June 25, 1995.
11. Croessman J. Street Machine Official Results. *Du Quoin Evening Call*. July 1, 1995.
12. Brauer K. Car Craft Held a Cruise and 9000 People Showed Up. *Hot Rod*. October 1995:91.
13. Kiewicz J. Car Craft Summer Cruise. *Car Craft*. October 1995:24-28.
14. Evans C. Central Park. For Street Machines, That Is. *Popular Hot Rodding*. October 1996:70-73.
15. Croessman J. Police Put NATs on 'Cruise Control'. *Du Quoin Evening Call*. June 22, 1996.

16. Croessman J. 100 Arrests During the NATs. *Du Quoin Evening Call*. June 24, 1996.
17. Croessman J. '67 Mustang, Graduation Present, Wins All the Marbles at '96 NATs. *Du Quoin Evening Call*. June 24, 1996.
18. Croessman J. Complete Results: Street Machine NATs Winners. *Du Quoin Evening Call*. June 26, 1996.
19. Fish R. The Nationals Stunk? *Popular Hot Rodding*. December 1996:7.
20. Summers B. Saturday Comment. *Du Quoin Evening Call*. June 29, 1996.
21. Evans C. Old School Fun. *Popular Hot Rodding*. November 1997:82-86.
22. Lenzi R. 1997 Miss Street Machine Nationals. Personal communication: Email. June 17, 2012.
23. Evans C. End of an Era. *Popular Hot Rodding*. November 1998:52-56.
24. Evans C. Big Changes for Du Quoin. *Popular Hot Rodding*. June 1998:8.
25. Evans C. Jammin' in Joliet. *Popular Hot Rodding*. October 1999:64-68.
26. Street Machines just good ol' American Fun. *The Daily Egyptian*. July 15, 1998.
27. Ziemba S. Drag Race Has Police Raising Red Flags. *Chicago Tribune*. June 29, 1999.
28. Hubley B. Founder and CEO of Family Events, Inc. Personal communication: Telephone interview. May 22, 2012.
29. Schifsky C. Former Editor, Car Craft. Personal communication: Telephone interview. May 27, 2011.
30. Baechtel J. Former staffer, Car Craft and Hot Rod Magazines. Personal communication: Telephone interview. May 19. 2011.
31. Smith J. Automotive journalist, former editor of Car Craft and Hot Rod. Personal communication: Telephone interview. May 12, 2011.

## chapter 15 | DON'T GO AWAY MAD (JUST GO AWAY)

32. Family Events. 2004 Street Machine Nationals Results. http://web.archive.org/web/20051125073630/http://www.familyevents.com/results/results.asp?c=1&i=15. Accessed March 16, 2012.

# chapter 16

# DON'T KNOW WHAT YOU GOT (TILL IT'S GONE)

Marc Telder photo

# chapter 16 | DON'T KNOW WHAT YOU GOT (TILL IT'S GONE)

*I can't tell ya baby what went wrong*
*I can't make you feel what you felt so long ago*
*I'll let it show*
*I can't give you back what's been hurt*
*Heartaches come and go and all that's left are the words*
*I can't let go*
*If we take some time to think it over baby*
*Take some time, let me know*
*If you really want to go*

*Don't know what you got till it's gone*
*Don't know what it is I did so wrong*
*Now I know what I got*
*It's just this song*
*And it ain't easy to get back*
*Takes so long*

"Don't Know What You Got (Till It's Gone)" by TC Keifer; © copyright 1988, Warner/Chappell Music, Inc.[1]

## It's SO Over

After thirteen years, the Du Quoin State Fairgrounds slammed the gates on the Street Machine Nationals for what would be—as far as we all knew—the final time in 1998. Show detractors had resisted the event before it had ever come to town in 1986. Their opposition steadily grew over the years.

Eventually they got their way.

Proponents of the event weren't about to let the annual gearhead rite of passage go down without a fight. Those who wanted the show to continue in Du Quoin generally fell into two camps. First, there were folks who sought to place blame. To them, maybe it was the crusty old conservatives in Du Quoin who were too stodgy to allow such revelry to continue in their streets. Or maybe it was the greedy magazines who had pulled their coverage of the event in 1994 so they could prop up their own competing shows. Or perhaps it was the partiers themselves who had used burnouts and booze to give the event its skanky reputation in the eyes of so many townsfolk.

The other group of supporters were far less vocal but no less passionate. To them, the loss of the Street Machine Nationals was a painful forfeiture of a once-cherished piece of their youth. Many of us had grown up at the Nats. Some had networked and forged lifelong friendships beneath the swaying leaves of the fairground trees. Others had built their livelihoods in the street machine scene with roots reaching deep into the show. It was a morose and somber and painful thing to see such an important bit of our lives simply wither and die.

Come June of 1999, no street machines stormed the fairground gates. There would be no revolution to overthrow the town's authorities. What happened instead was no less remarkable.

Nothing.

Nothing at all happened. Over time, the Fairgrounds would attract other events. There were large livestock and equine shows. There were travel trailer shows and agriculture, hunting, and fishing expositions. With the opening of the 3,000-seat Southern Illinois Center in 2005, monster truck shows, motocross, and indoor dirt track racing came to town.[2] Tantalizingly, local car shows—tiny in size compared to the Nats—would occupy a microscopic corner of the grounds one Saturday a year.[3]

But virtually no sign remained of the fact that the place had served as ground zero of the pro street revolution and the Greatest Show on Wheels for more than a decade.

Shut down. Shut out. Homeless.

It was probably for the best. Things had gotten that bad.

## chapter 16 | DON'T KNOW WHAT YOU GOT (TILL IT'S GONE)

After the brief stop in Indy and the forgettable two years in Lima, event organizers decided enough was enough. They pulled the plug for what everyone thought was the very last time.[4,5]

Oh, how the mighty had fallen.

However, despite the death of a once proud and expansive automotive car show franchise, it wasn't like other car shows weren't thriving. You couldn't blame Special Events. Although the Nats had apparently died out, several of their other shows had continued to grow. For example, the Car Craft Magazine Summer Nationals in Minneapolis, Minnesota, had flourished into a dependable annual gathering of 5,000 cars. The Hot Rod Power Tour had become wildly popular, as well.

The Power Tour was arguably the brainchild of Jeff Smith and later others at *Hot Rod* with the "Victory Tours" in the early '90s. Within the pages of the magazine, staffers would detail four-day hauls in high caliber street machines from Du Quoin to points west, often with stops in different towns along the way each year.

Officially launched in 1995, the Power Tour has grown into an impressive event in its own right, attracting around 5,400 participants and more than 85,000 spectators in 2012 alone.[6,7] The "rolling tribute to the performance car" annually involves five or six different tour stops, cruising from town to town each day as "the ultimate gearhead roadtrip."[7] No two years of the Tour are the same, with a different lineup of stops announced annually. The Tour even stopped in Du Quoin in 2010.[7,8]

Over the span of two decades, it steadily overtook the original Street Machine Nationals in terms of participation and popularity. The mind-boggling logistics involved in hosting a five-day long car show scattered across a dozen states and 1,500 miles are expertly handled by Family Events staff Michael Moore, Ron Carlson, Jessica Hubley (founder Bruce's daughter), Matthew Louck, and a talented and committed handful of others.

Other non-Family Events shows like the Goodguys' show series have also grown in popularity. Like the Summer Nationals and the Power Tour, these events were increasingly popular gatherings of impressive numbers of hot rods and street machines. However, they weren't strictly about pub-

lic display of raunchy behavior in the presence of cool cars. They were and continue to be about friends and family in the presence of performing cars.

"Back then, we used to just park our cars, party, and sit around all weekend," said longtime show participant Bret Voelkel. Save for fairgrounds cruising, Voelkel was right. "Today, we get to drive our cars at events like the Power Tour and compete in the Autocross Challenge and the Wilwood Speed Stop Challenges and such. It is a lot more fun to get in the car and drive it than it is to just sit around," he added.[9]

Arguably, the movement away from the largely passive fairgrounds scene of the '80s and '90s toward more participation-based events of today might have actually started in retaliation to the fairground queen pro street cars that dominated the landscape back in the day. This new breed of shows offered more than just shaded acres for parking cars. They actually encouraged participants *to participate*.

It was undoubtedly the "other stuff" that surrounded these new events that made them so much more refined and appealing to a maturing audience. And that, in turn, made them appealing to the towns that might potentially host them. In a change of pace compared to the Nats, the buying power and economic impact of the incoming crowd was no longer offset by how much the gathered crowd tore up while they were there.

The Nats had offered stationary show & shine. As Voelkel pointed out, newer automotive events offered autocross, quick stop braking challenges, sanctioned burnout contests, and on-site dyno testing. The Nats had a high proportion of partiers and regular displays of public nudity. New shows had jumping castles and "Make-N-Take" model building for the kids. Times had changed.

What these new events recognized that the Nats simply hadn't was that we all eventually grew up. It wasn't cool for a 40+ year old guy to roll out of an unfamilar bed on Sunday morning with no recollection of how he ended up there or what on Earth he had done the night before. And as pointed out by legendary builder Rocky Robertson, no one was interested in seeing an aging female willing to bare her down-trending anterior assets as she cruised by on the deck of an old convertible. Just—*no*.

# chapter 16 | DON'T KNOW WHAT YOU GOT (TILL IT'S GONE)

Now that the show is back, hopes are high that it will be a regular on the Family Events summer schedule. However, Du Quoin State Fairgrounds and Family Events representatives have both repeatedly stated that while a return is possible, no commitment beyond 2013 yet exists.[4,10] Everyone involved seems guardedly optimistic that those who show up to the event can be reasonably well behaved. The fingers-crossed desire is that it can grow and flourish into all the best things it used to be. Simply put, there will be no third chance.

The earnest hope of most is that we have all managed to learn our lessons from the past. The new and improved version of the show will feature those family-friendly and participant-based attractions that have proven to be popular in contemporary events. Furthermore, Du Quoin residents and the city's own *Evening Call* have shown genuine interest in the return of the show. It can be, as it once was, a great event in a great facility that happens to be in a great little small town.

## *Glory Days*

*Now I think I'm going down to the well tonight*
*And I'm going to drink 'till I get my fill*
*And I hope when I get old I don't sit around thinking about it*
*But I probably will*
*Yeah, just sitting back trying to recapture*
*A little of the glory of, well time slips away*
*And leaves you with nothing mister but*
*Boring stories of glory days*

*Glory days well they'll pass you by*
*Glory days in the wink of a young girl's eye*
*Glory days, glory days*

"Glory Days" by B. Springsteen; © copyright 1985, Universal Music Publishing Group.[11]

Something happened as the Nats aged and changed: so too did the people who originally attended and participated. By the time the show left Du Quoin after 1998, scarce few of those in the crowd fully understood the history of the event. Du Quoin seemed pretty happy to live life without the hassle, those who loved street machines found other venues, and partiers found new parties. Life went on.

The estimated economic impact of the 1998 Street Machine Nationals was typically cited as somewhere between $15-$16.5 million dollars.[12] Based on that estimate and adjusting for inflation, the net loss to the Southern Illinois economy as a result of shuttering an annual event like the Nats is now over $2.7 billion. In light of the State of Illinois' horrific economic woes, that's money that would have been spent pretty easily in exchange for three days of inconvenience each year.

Unemployment in Southern Illinois has historically outpaced national averages. From 1998 until 2009, that rate has fluctuated between 4.4 and 8.5%.[13] However, that number jumped to 9.0% in March 2009 and has been at or above 10% ever since, even going to 11.3% in February, 2010.[13]

The State Fairgrounds haven't been immune to the economic pinch either. Talk around the Illinois capitol in Springfield in 2009 was that the State could no longer foot the bill for one—let alone two—state fairs as Illinois has had for nearly a century. The fairs had cost Illinois taxpayers nearly $42 million between 2001 and 2009 alone and Illinois was in no position to continue to pick up the tab.[14] Although the proverbial shows have gone on, it has not been without considerable public debate and political posturing.

That's probably why the timing for the show's return could not have been better. Thousands of former participants and spectators have managed to reconnect and begin discussions about how great it would be to get together again. And just like the lyrics Springsteen penned nearly 20 years ago, we want to get together and sit back, trying to recapture "boring stories" of our very own glory days.

Meanwhile, cash-strapped Illinois—specifically Du Quoin—sees the potential in the return of a kinder, gentler Street Machine Nationals. Much-needed tax and sales revenue would be helpful in covering needs that have gone unmet due to financial constraints.[10]

Make no mistake—there are still concerns. As recently as late May, the Du Quoin City Council passed three local ordinances aimed at controlling crowds and crimes at the show for 2013.[15] Most controversial was a ban on cruising that has led many to question whether Du Quoin's arms have really been reopened quite as wide as first thought.

Ordinances aside, 2013 marks the show's return. It might have taken years, but townsfolk are finally willing to risk the possible downside in order to host it all again. With planning, praying, and a little bit of luck, the show will go off without incident and we can all come to count on it again in future summers.

For all that it was and for all that it is, the Street Machine Nationals were a cultural phenomenon the likes of which middle America—and eventually the world—had never seen. Whether it was the spectacle of 5,000 cars crammed into the fairgrounds at Indy or 3,800 cars sprinkled amongst the trees and lakes and hills in Du Quoin, it was incomparable. Maybe it was the overpowering visual assault of neon, chrome, billet, and bikinis. Or maybe the sound of Pete Jackson gear drives, overdriven superchargers, and roasting rear tires. Or maybe even the smell of spent $6-a-gallon race gas, burning rubber, or 100,000 sunburns in the Southern Illinois heat (trust me, that has a smell too). Regardless, it was unsurpassed awesomeness and sensory overload in every sense of the term.

It was real.

And it was *spectacular*.

## References

1. Lyrics007.com. Don't Know What You Got (Till It's Gone) lyrics. http://www.lyrics007.com/Cinderella Lyrics/Don't Know What You Got (Till It's Gone) Lyrics.html. Accessed May 19, 2013.
2. North American Motorsports. Southern Illinois Center. 2013; http://www.na-motorsports.com/Tracks/IL/SouthernIllinoisCenter.html. Accessed May 12, 2013.
3. Mason J. Executive I, Illinois Department of Agriculture, Du Quoin State Fair. Personal communication: Telephone interview. May 20, 2011.
4. Hubley B. Founder and CEO of Family Events, Inc. Personal communication: Telephone interview. May 22, 2012.
5. Davis S. Former Director, Special Events. Personal communication: Telephone interview. May 12, 2012.
6. Hardin D. Join Us On Our Power Tour. *Hot Rod*. February 1995:7.
7. Hot Rod Magazine. Hot Rod Power Tour. 2013; http://www.hotrod.com/2013/powertour/. Accessed March 19, 2013.
8. Croessman JH. Hot Rod Magazine Power Tour in Du Quoin Monday. *Du Quoin Evening Call*. June 4, 2010.
9. Voelkel B. RideTech Founder. Personal communication: Telephone interview. April 17, 2012.
10. John Rednour J. Director, Du Quoin State Fair. Personal communication: Telephone interview. April 13, 2013.
11. LyricsDepot.com. Glory Days lyrics. http://www.lyricsdepot.com/bruce-springsteen/glory-days.html. Accessed May 20, 2013.
12. Family Events. 22nd Annual Street Machine Nationals. 1998; http://www.web.archive.org/web/19991009165143/http://family-events.com/1998Events/98-dequoin-results.html. Accessed March 17, 2012.

13. Bureau of Labor Statistics. Historical unemployment data by region and date. 2013; http://data.bls.gov/pdq/SurveyOutputServlet Accessed May 17, 2013.
14. Illinois Policy Institute. Spotlight on Spending #9: The State UnFair. July 29, 2010.
15. WSIL-TV. Du Quoin Concerned About Safety During Street Machine Nationals. May 22, 2013; http://www.wsiltv.com/news/local/Du-Quoin-Concerned-About-Safety-During-Street-Machine-Nationals-208564101.html, May 29, 2013.

# appendices

# Appendix A: Builder Bios

## APPENDICES

| | Year | Make | Model | Mo/Yr | Mag | Name | Description |
|---|---|---|---|---|---|---|---|
| Richard Boyd | 1978 | Chevy | Camaro | Nov-83 | Hot Rod | Sizzlers | Black, graphics, blown, tubbed |
| | 1978 | Chevy | Camaro | Nov-84 | PHR | Double Take | Yellow, blown, tubbed |
| | 1978 | Chevy | Camaro | Apr-85 | Hot Rod | Colorfast | Yellow, blown, tubbed |
| | 1978 | Chevy | Camaro | Oct-85 | Car Craft | | Yellow, blown, tubbed |
| | 1968 | Chevy | Camaro | Jul-88 | PHR | Heartbeat | Yellow, blown, tubbed |
| | 1978 | Chevy | Camaro | Jun-90 | Hot Rod | Shock Treatment | Yellow, blown, tubbed |
| | 1985 | Chevy | Camaro | Oct-91 | Car Craft | Old Yeller | Yellow, tubbed, blown SBC |
| | 1985 | Chevy | Camaro | Oct-91 | PHR | Sweet Revenge | Yellow, tubbed, blown SBC |
| | 1985 | Chevy | Camaro | Dec-92 | Hot Rod | Blown Away | Yellow, tubbed, blown SBC |
| Rick Dobbertin | 1965 | Chevy | Nova | Sep-82 | Hot Rod | Overkill (cover) | HR Street Machine of the Year '82; Best of the Decade |
| | 1965 | Chevy | Nova | Oct-82 | Car Craft | Grand champion, 82 nats | |
| | 1965 | Chevy | Nova | Oct-82 | PHR | Nova to go with Everything | |
| | | | | Feb-84 | Car Craft | Prince of Pro Street | |
| | 1985 | Pontiac | J-2000 | Aug-86 | Car Craft | One Step Beyond | The J-2000; Top 10 March 97 |
| | 1985 | Pontiac | J-2000 | Sep-86 | Car Craft | One Step Beyond Pt. 2 | J-2000 buildup |
| | 1985 | Pontiac | J-2000 | Oct-86 | PHR | Top Gun | 10 best ever PHR July 89 |
| | 1985 | Pontiac | J-2000 | Oct-86 | Hot Rod | Out Radical Rageous | 1986 Hot Rod of the Year; Best of the Decade |
| | 1988 | Pontiac | Grand Am | Aug-88 | Hot Rod | Front drive | |
| | 1988 | Pontiac | Grand Am | Nov-88 | Car Craft | Kings of Pro Street | White daily driver pro street |
| | 1985 | Pontiac | J-2000 | Aug-95 | Hot Rod | Ten Best Street Machines of All Time | 1986 Hot Rod of the Year; Best of the Decade |
| Elder | 1970 | Dodge | Challenger | Feb-90 | Hot Rod | Mo-Genta | Pink, blown, tubbed |
| | 1970 | Dodge | Challenger | Oct-91 | PHR | Bad to the Bone | Red, tubbed, tube chassis, blown & injected hemi; HR top 10 |
| | 1970 | Dodge | Challenger | Dec-91 | Hot Rod | Blown Away | Red, tubbed, tube chassis, blown & injected hemi; HR top 10 |
| S. Gantz | 1965 | Dodge | Coronet | Oct-89 | Hot Rod | Wedge-O-Matic | Maroon, tubbed |
| | 1965 | Dodge | Coronet | May-90 | Car Craft | Prairie Prowler | Maroon, tubbed |
| | 1965 | Chevy | Corvette | Sep-96 | Hot Rod | Pro Low is So Low | Red, tubbed, cammer SBC; Top 10 Street Machine March 97 |
| | 1965 | Chevy | Corvette | Oct-96 | PHR | American Dream | Red, tubbed, cammer SBC; Top 10 Street Machine March 97 |
| | 1965 | Chevy | Corvette | Dec-96 | Car Craft | The Outer Limit | Red, tubbed, cammer SBC; Top 10 Street Machine March 97 |
| Rich Gebhardt | 1982 | Chevy | Monte Carlo | Jan-86 | PHR | PD Quick | Injected BBC, full tube chassis |
| | 1986 | Chevy | Cavalier | Nov-86 | PHR | Pretty Darn Quik | Injected BBC, full tube chassis |
| | 1984 | Chevy | Cavalier | Dec-86 | Car Craft | Cavalier Attitude | Injected BBC, full tube chassis. Blue and silver |
| | 1984 | Chevy | Cavalier | Dec-86 | Hot Rod | Z-Wiz | |
| | 1989 | Chevy | Beretta | Oct-89 | Hot Rod | Ballistic Beretta | Orange V6 full tube; HR top 10 '89 |
| | 1989 | Chevy | Beretta | Nov-89 | Car Craft | Original Condition | Orange V6 full tube |
| | 1987 | Ford | Tempo | Jan-90 | Hot Rod | Tempo-rary Insanity | Blue, Gebhardt built |
| | 1988 | Chevy | Cavalier | Feb-90 | Car Craft | Pro-Gressive | Gebhardt built; Red, tube chassis, injected SBC |
| | | | | Apr-90 | Car Craft | Hi-Riser: Rich Gebhardt | |
| | | | | Apr-90 | Hot Rod | The Pro Shop | |
| | 1989 | Chevy | Beretta | Apr-90 | PHR | Tuned Port Terror | Blue, TPI, Gebhardt built |
| | 1990 | Oldsmobile | Cutlass | Sep-90 | PHR | Oh So Bad | Blue, Gebhardt built, BBC |
| | 1990 | Oldsmobile | Cutlass | Nov-90 | Hot Rod | Street Slasher Supreme | Blue, Gebhardt built, BBC |
| | 1989 | Chevy | Cavalier | Jan-91 | Hot Rod | Red Menace | Gebhardt-built; Sullivan Graphics |
| | 1990 | Oldsmobile | Cutlass | Mar-91 | Car Craft | Pro Archetype | Blue, Gebhardt built, BBC |
| | 1988 | Chevy | Camaro | Apr-92 | Car Craft | Factory Fresh | Red, tubbed, tunnel rammed BBC; Gebhardt chassis |
| | 1970 | Poniac | GTO | Oct-92 | Hot Rod | True Believer | Purple, tubbed, tunnel ram, Gebhardt built |
| | 1970 | Poniac | GTO | Nov-92 | PHR | Pro Purple | Purple, tubbed, tunnel ram, Gebhardt built |
| | 1970 | Poniac | GTO | Nov-92 | Car Craft | Purple Haze | Purple, tubbed, tunnel ram, Gebhardt built |
| | 1993 | Pontiac | Grand Am | Dec-93 | Car Craft | Warning Sign | Yellow, blown, tube chassis, Gebhardt |
| | 1989 | Chevy | Cavalier | Feb-94 | Car Craft | Cavalier Attitude | Orange, tube chassis, Gebhardt built |
| | 1994 | Pontiac | Trans Am | Nov-94 | Car Craft | Good As Gold | Purple, blown LT-1, Gebhardt backhalf |
| | 1993 | Pontiac | Grand Prix | Dec-94 | PHR | Poncho Cheese | Yellow, tube chassis, BBC, Gebhardt built |
| Merle Goldesberry | 1990 | Chevy | Beretta | Dec-91 | Car Craft | Blue Flame | Blue, tunnel rammed SBC; Cover car |
| | 1964 | Plymouth | Biscaine | Jan-92 | Car Craft | Straight Scoop Garage | |
| | 1993 | Pontiac | Grand Am | Apr-93 | Car Craft | Straight Scoop Garage | |
| | 1993 | Pontiac | Grand Am | Dec-93 | Car Craft | Warning Sign | Yellow, blown, tube chassis, Gebhardt |
| | 1989 | Chevy | Cavalier | Feb-94 | Car Craft | Cavalier Attitude | Orange, tube chassis, Gebhardt built |
| | 1994 | Pontiac | Trans Am | May-94 | Car Craft | Straight Scoop Garage | |
| | 1994 | Pontiac | Trans Am | Oct-94 | PHR | Prone Street | Purple, blown LT-1, Gebhardt backhalf |
| | 1994 | Pontiac | Trans Am | Nov-94 | Car Craft | Good As Gold | Purple, blown LT-1, Gebhardt backhalf |
| | 1996 | Pontiac | Sunfire | Mar-96 | Car Craft | Sun Inferno | Tube chassis, Blown BBCm red w/ flames |

259

## Appendix A: Builder Bios

| Builder | Year | Make | Model | Date | Mag | Title | Notes |
|---|---|---|---|---|---|---|---|
| Mark Grimes | 1972 | Chevy | Vega | Sep-83 | Hot Rod | SM Nats show coverage | |
| | 1972 | Chevy | Vega | Nov-83 | PHR | Great Plains Drifters | Light blue, tubbed, blown BBC |
| | 1972 | Chevy | Vega | Jan-85 | Car Craft | Azure Like It | Light blue, tubbed, blown BBC |
| | 1965 | Chevy | Malibu | Nov-86 | PHR | Pro One | PHR 10 Best Ever |
| | 1965 | Chevy | Malibu | Nov-86 | Hot Rod | Maliblue Thunder | |
| | 1965 | Chevy | Malibu | Dec-87 | Car Craft | America's Best Street Machine? | Blown & injected, tubbed, blue, COVER; Top 10 March 97 |
| | 1987 | Chevy | Eurosport | Oct-88 | PHR | Overblown | Cover car; 10 best of all time PHR July 89 |
| | 1987 | Chevy | Eurosport | Oct-88 | Hot Rod | Red, White, & Blown | Red Eurosport |
| | 1987 | Chevy | Eurosport | Nov-88 | Car Craft | Kings of Pro Street | Red Eurosport |
| | | | | Apr-90 | Car Craft | Transportation Transformation | |
| | 1962 | Chevy | Nova | Oct-92 | Car Craft | Nouveau Nova | Pro street/pro touring style |
| | 1962 | Chevy | Nova | Mar-93 | Hot Rod | Nouveau Nova | Pro street/pro touring style |
| | 1968 | Cadillac | Convertible | Feb-94 | Hot Rod | Preview of Caddy Attractions | Tubbed convertible |
| | 1968 | Cadillac | Convertible | Oct-94 | PHR | Black Barge | Tubbed convertible |
| Matt & Debbie Hay | 1966 | Ford | Mustang | Nov-78 | Hot Rod | The Wild Bunch | Blown SBC |
| | 1966 | Ford | Mustang | Oct-79 | PHR | Half Breed | Blown SBC; tubbed |
| | 1979 | Ford | Mustang | Sep-83 | Hot Rod | SMNats show coverage | |
| | 1979 | Ford | Mustang | Nov-83 | PHR | Half Breed | The Mustang; COVER |
| | 1979 | Ford | Mustang | Feb-84 | Car Craft | Haulin' Oats | The Mustang; COVER |
| | 1984 | Oldsmobile | Ciera | Nov-85 | Hot Rod | Who's Kidding Who? | The Olds; Dec 1985 HR Top 10 |
| | 1984 | Oldsmobile | Ciera | Jun-86 | Car Craft | Vision Quest | The Olds |
| | 1988 | Ford | Thunderbird | Nov-88 | Hot Rod | Too Bad T-Bird | Pink T-Bird (Top 10) |
| | 1988 | Ford | Thunderbird | Nov-88 | Car Craft | Kings of Pro Street | Pink T-Bird |
| | 1988 | Ford | Thunderbird | Jul-89 | PHR | Hay Hay Take it Away | PHR 10 Best Ever July 89 |
| Al Hinds | 1980 | Chevy | Camaro | Feb-89 | PHR | Camaros | Tubbed, blown, injected |
| | 1989 | Chevy | Beretta | Dec-90 | Car Craft | Beretta, Eh? | Green, full tube, blown & injected |
| | 1989 | Chevy | Beretta | Mar-91 | Hot Rod | Hindsight | Green, full tube, blown & injected |
| | 1991 | Chevy | Lumina | Apr-91 | Car Craft | Straight Scoop Garage | Build photos |
| | 1992 | Chevy | Lumina | Oct-92 | Hot Rod | Zoomina! | Blue, blown, injected, tubbed |
| | 1992 | Chevy | Lumina | Nov-92 | Car Craft | Pro Street Shootout | Blue, blown, injected, tubbed |
| | 1991 | Chevy | Lumina | Aug-92 | Car Craft | Northern Exposure | Blue, blown, injected, tubbed: Top Ten Street Machine March 97 |
| | 1991 | Chevy | Lumina | Nov-92 | PHR | Green Light | Blue, blown, injected, tubbed: Top Ten Street Machine March 97 |
| Maynard | 1971 | Chevy | Camaro | Nov-90 | Hot Rod | Out of the Blue | Inline 6, tubbed, aqua |
| | 1971 | Chevy | Camaro | May-91 | Car Craft | Pro Street Sixation | Inline 6, tubbed, aqua |
| | 1961 | Dodge | Seneca | Dec-94 | Car Craft | | |
| Rocky Robertson | 1969 | Chevy | Nova | Jun-86 | PHR | Street Lethal | Cover, red, tubbed |
| | 1985 | Buick | Somerset | Nov-86 | Hot Rod | Prom Queen | Cover; Hot Rod Top Ten 1986 |
| | 1985 | Buick | Somerset | Mar-87 | Car Craft | Roadmaster | Turbo V-6 |
| | 1985 | Buick | Somerset | Jun-87 | PHR | Rapid Red Rocket | Turbo V-6 |
| | 1988 | Buick | LeSabre | Nov-88 | Hot Rod | LeSabre Rattling | Pink, injected V6 |
| | 1988 | Buick | LeSabre | Mar-90 | Car Craft | Look Sharp | Pink, injected V6 |
| | | | | May-90 | Car Craft | Future Street | |
| | 1988 | Buick | LeSabre | Nov-90 | PHR | Run'n Low | 10 Best Ever PHR July 89 |
| | 1951 | Kaiser | Coupe | Nov-94 | Hot Rod | Rollin' with Rocky | Flamed, stainless chassis |
| | 1951 | Kaiser | Coupe | Dec-94 | Hot Rod | Rocky's Roller | Flamed, stainless chassis |
| Rod Saboury | 1969 | Chevy | Camaro | Jan-78 | Car Craft | | Super stock |
| | 1969 | Chevy | Camaro | Oct-83 | Car Craft | The Changeling | Blown, injected, tubbed COVER |
| | 1969 | Chevy | Camaro | Nov-83 | PHR | It's For Real | Blown, injected, tubbed |
| | 1969 | Chevy | Camaro | Dec-83 | Hot Rod | Hot Rods of Today | Blown, injected, tubbed |
| | 1963 | Chevy | Corvette | Jul-86 | PHR | Potent Pair | Blown BBC, Black split window; PHR 10 best ever July 89 |
| | 1963 | Chevy | Corvette | Apr-87 | Car Craft | The Sting | Blown BBC, Black split window |
| | 1959 | Chevy | Corvette | Apr-91 | Car Craft | Supercharged Supercar | Blown BBC, burgundy |
| | 1967 | Chevy | Camaro | Jun-90 | Car Craft | Tang-Go | Rod Saboury built frame, blown, tubbed |
| | 1959 | Chevy | Corvette | Mar-91 | Hot Rod | vette threat | Brown, blown BBC |
| | 1957 | Chevy | Corvette | Sep-92 | Hot Rod | 10 Fastest Street Cars | White, multi-colored graphics |
| | 1957 | Chevy | Corvette | Nov-92 | Car Craft | Pro Street Shootout | White, multi-colored graphics |
| | 1957 | Chevy | Corvette | Feb-93 | Hot Rod | The Corvette that Eight Memphis | White, multi-colored graphics |
| | 1957 | Chevy | Corvette | Aug-93 | Car Craft | First Street Car in the 6's | White, multi-colored graphics |
| | 1957 | Chevy | Corvette | Apr-95 | PHR | World's Fastest '57 | White, multi-colored graphics |
| | 1953 | Chevy | Corvette | Jan-98 | PHR | The Outlaw | White, multi-colored graphics |

260

# Appendix A: Builder Bios

## Scott Sullivan

| Year | Make | Model | Date | Magazine | Title | Notes |
|---|---|---|---|---|---|---|
| 1967 | Chevy | Nova | Oct-79 | Car Craft | | THE car; Top 10 March 97; |
| 1967 | Chevy | Nova | Oct-79 | Hot Rod | | Street Machine of the Year |
| 1967 | Chevy | Nova | Oct-79 | PHR | Pro Street Super Sport | |
| 1964 | Chevy | Nova | Feb-87 | Hot Rod | Smooth & Subtle | Beige, inline 6 |
| 1967 | Chevy | Nova | Sep-87 | Hot Rod | Giveaway | |
| 1955 | Chevy | Bel Air | Dec-88 | Hot Rod | Pro Interstate | Top 10 (Hot Rod); Best of the Decade |
| 1955 | Chevy | Bel Air | Jan-89 | Hot Rod | Pro Interstate Part 2 | Top 10 (Hot Rod) |
| 1957 | Chevy | Belair | Jun-93 | Hot Rod | The Magnificent Obsession | Top 10 1993 |
| 1955 | Chevy | Bel Air | Aug-95 | Hot Rod | Ten Best Street Machines | "Will go down in history as one of the nicest cars ever built." |
| 1967 | Chevy | Nova | Aug-95 | Hot Rod | Ten Best Street Machine | THE car; Top 10 March 97 |
| 1969 | Chevy | Camaro | Mar-79 | Car Craft | | Scott Sullivan painted |
| 1970 | Chevy | Chevelle | Mar-79 | Car Craft | | Scott Sullivan painted |
| 1970 | Chevy | Chevelle | Sep-80 | Hot Rod | | Scott Sullivan built |
| 1970 | Chevy | Chevelle | Oct-80 | Hot Rod | | Scott Sullivan built |
| 1966 | Chevy | Chevelle | Sep-85 | Hot Rod | Industrial Strength | Sullivan graphics |
| 1970 | Chevy | Nova | Jun-86 | Car Craft | Avante Guard | Blue pro street; Sullivan graphics |
| 1966 | Chevy | Chevelle | Sep-86 | Car Craft | Under Cover Mission | Pale blue, blown, tubbed, Sullivan graphics |
| 1933 | Ford | Coupe | Jun-88 | Hot Rod | Scott Sullivan built | |
| 1989 | Chevy | Beretta | Dec-89 | PHR | Power Play | Sullivan graphics; PHR top 10 of the year |
| 1989 | Chevy | Beretta | Dec-89 | Hot Rod | Green Beretta | Sullivan graphics |
| 1956 | Chevy | Pickup | Nov-90 | Hot Rod | Pickup From Heaven | Sullivan graphics |
| 1986 | Chevy | Camaro | Dec-90 | Hot Rod | Orange peeler | Cheese whiz orange; Sullivan graphics |
| 1989 | Chevy | Beretta | Dec-90 | Car Craft | Beretta, Eh? | Green, full tube, blown & injected; Sullivan graphics on hood |
| 1989 | Chevy | Cavalier | Jan-91 | Hot Rod | Red Menace | Gebhardt-built; Sullivan Graphics |
| 1937 | Ford | Coupe | Mar-91 | Hot Rod | Rolling the Dice | Sullivan Graphics |
| 1989 | Chevy | Beretta | Mar-91 | Hot Rod | Hindsight | Green, full tube, blown & injected; Sullivan graphics on hood |
| 1978 | Chevy | Camaro | May-91 | Hot Rod | A Cool Guy's Camaro | Sullivan graphics |
| 1974 | Chevy | Camaro | Aug-91 | Hot Rod | Pro Home-Built | tubbed, Sullivan graphics |
| 1986 | Chevy | Pickup | Feb-93 | Hot Rod | Truckin' on Down | Sullivan graphics |
| 1968 | Chevy | Camaro | Nov-93 | Hot Rod | Dem Bones | Purple & blue, tubbed, Sullivan graphics |
| 1968 | Chevy | Camaro | Feb-94 | Car Craft | Bad to the Bone | Purple & blue, tubbed, Sullivan graphics |
| 1974 | Plymouth | Road Runner | Feb-95 | PHR | Fine Whine | Sullivan graphics |
| 1986 | Chevy | Pickup | Mar-95 | PHR | Perfectly Pleasant | Sullivan graphics |

## Danny Taylor

| Year | Make | Model | Date | Magazine | Title | Notes |
|---|---|---|---|---|---|---|
| 1979 | Chevy | Malibu | Oct-83 | PHR | Kentucky Candy | Yellow, chopped top |
| 1981 | Buick | Regal | Jun-86 | Car Craft | Graphic Example | Blue/purple; Taylor painted |
| 1978 | Chevy | Malibu | Oct-87 | Hot Rod | Multi-Hue Malibu | White, red, tubbed |
| 1978 | Chevy | Malibu | Jul-88 | PHR | 90 Day Wonder | White, red, tubbed |
| 1979 | Chevy | Malibu | Jan-90 | Hot Rod | Double Vision | Blue street machine |
| 1979 | Pontiac | LeMans | Jan-90 | Hot Rod | Double Vision | Pink street machine |
| 1983 | Chevy | Malibu | Dec-89 | PHR | | PHR top 10 of the year |
| 1983 | Chevy | Malibu | Mar-90 | Car Craft | High Impact | Yellow, tubbed, Danny Taylor graphics |
| 1978 | Chevy | Malibu | Jun-90 | Car Craft | Big Shoebox to Fill | White, blown, tubbed |
| 1979 | Pontiac | LeMans | Jun-90 | Car Craft | Kentucky Blue Streak | Danny Taylor painted |
| 1983 | Chevy | Malibu | Jun-90 | Hot Rod | Screaming Yellow 'Bu | Yellow, tubbed, Danny Taylor graphics |
| 1978 | Chevy | Malibu | Oct-91 | Car Craft | Taylormade | White, black, pink, aqua |
| 1978 | Chevy | Malibu | Jan-92 | PHR | Malibu Magic | White, black, pink, aqua |
| 1978 | Chevy | Malibu | Feb-92 | Hot Rod | Malibrew | White, black, pink, aqua |

# Appendix A: Builder Bios

| | Year | Make | Model | Date | Mag | Title | Notes |
|---|---|---|---|---|---|---|---|
| Troy Trepanier | 1966 | Chevy | Chevelle | Sep-87 | PHR | Low Approach | Red, blown, tubbed |
| | 1966 | Chevy | Chevelle | Oct-88 | Hot Rod | Hot Pink | Raspberry, blown, tubbed |
| | 1966 | Chevy | Chevelle | Nov-88 | PHR | Out to Launch | Raspberry, blown, tubbed |
| | 1966 | Chevy | Chevelle | Jan-89 | Car Craft | Razz-A-Ma-Tazz | Raspberry, blown, tubbed |
| | | | | Apr-90 | Car Craft | Transportation Transformation | |
| | 1960 | Chevy | Impala | Sep-90 | Hot Rod | Greenhouse Effect | Wintermint green probox; 1990 Hot Rod of the Year |
| | 1960 | Chevy | Impala | Oct-90 | PHR | Troy's Toy | Wintermint green probox |
| | 1960 | Chevy | Impala | Nov-90 | Car Craft | Grand Slammed | Wintermint green probox |
| | 1950 | Buick | Roadmaster | Jan-92 | Hot Rod | Troy Boy's New Toy | |
| | 1950 | Buick | Roadmaster | Jun-92 | Car Craft | Build pics | |
| | 1950 | Buick | Roadmaster | Aug-92 | Car Craft | Leviathan | Peach & root beer; injected, tubbed; Top 10 March 97 |
| | 1950 | Buick | Roadmaster | Aug-92 | Hot Rod | Bumongous | Peach & root beer; injected, tubbed; Top 10 March 97 |
| | 1950 | Buick | Roadmaster | Dec-92 | PHR | 2 Big | Peach & root beer; injected, tubbed; Top 10 March 97 |
| | 1960 | Dodge | Rambler | Sep-94 | Hot Rod | Let's Rumble | Ramblur; HR Top 10 |
| | 1961 | Chevy | Biscaine | Oct-97 | Car Craft | Bisquik | Silver, pro touring style |
| | 1961 | Chevy | Biscaine | Oct-97 | PHR | Bisquik | Silver, pro touring style |
| | 1954 | Plymouth | Savoy | Dec-97 | Hot Rod | Bull's Eye | Pro touring; Sniper |
| | 1954 | Plymouth | Savoy | Feb-98 | Hot Rod | Bull's Eye Part II | Pro touring; Sniper |
| Bret Voelkel | 1970 | Ford | Mustang | Nov-84 | PHR | Mellow Yellow | |
| | 1970 | Ford | Mustang | Oct-86 | Car Craft | Cover car | |
| | 1979 | Ford | Fairmont | Nov-91 | Car Craft | Far-Out Fairmont | Blown, injected, red |
| | 1970 | Ford | Mustang | Oct-96 | PHR | Cover car | White & orange; first airride pro street |
| | 1970 | Ford | Mustang | Nov-96 | PHR | Hoosier Hauler | White & orange; first airride pro street |
| | 1970 | Ford | Mustang | Jan-97 | Hot Rod | Super 'Stang | White & orange; first airride pro street |

# Appendix B: Street Machine Nationals Year-By-Year Summary

|  | Year | Town | Date | Partic. | Spect. | #1 Song | #1 Movie |
|---|---|---|---|---|---|---|---|
| 1st | 1977 | Indianapolis, IN | June 24-26 | 1300+ | 10,000 | Dreams, Fleetwood Mac | The Rescuers |
| 2nd | 1978 | Indianapolis, IN | June 23-25 | 2538 | 25,000 | Shadow Dancing, Andy Gibb | Grease |
| 3rd | 1979 | Indianapolis, IN | June 22-24 | 4800 | 30,000 | Hot Stuff, Donna Summer | The Muppet Movie |
| 4th | 1980 | Indianapolis, IN | June 20-22 | 5000 | 30,000 | Coming Up, Paul McCartney & Wings | The Empire Strikes Back |
| 5th | 1981 | Indianapolis, IN | June 19-21 | 5000 | 60,000 | Bette Davis Eyes, Kim Carnes | For Your Eyes Only |
| 6th | 1982 | Springfield, IL | June 25-27 | 5000 | 75,000 | Ebony and Ivory, Paul McCartney & Stevie Wonder | E.T. |
| 7th | 1983 | Springfield, IL | June 24-26 | 5000 | 100,000 | Flashdance: Irene Cara | Return of the Jedi |
| 8th | 1984 | Springfield, IL | June 22-24 | 5000 | 113,000 | The Reflex, Duran Duran | Ghostbusters |
| 9th | 1985 | St. Louis, MO | June 28-30 | 4000 | 120,000 | Heaven, Brian Adams | Pale Rider |
| 10th | 1986 | DuQuoin, IL | June 27-29 | 3000 | 62,124 | On My Own, Patti LaBelle | Karate Kid 2 |
| 11th | 1987 | DuQuoin, IL | June 26-28 | 3000 | 65,000 | Head to Toe, Lisa Lisa | Dragnet |
| 12th | 1988 | DuQuoin, IL | June 24-26 | 3485 | 61,000 | Together Forever, Rick Astley | Who Framed Roger Rabbit |
| 13th | 1989 | DuQuoin, IL | June 23-25 | 3562 | 101,000 | I'll Be Loving You Forever, New Kids on the Block | Batman |
| 14th | 1990 | DuQuoin, IL | June 22-24 | 3620 | 106,865 | It Must Have Been Love, Roxette | Days of Thunder |
| 15th | 1991 | DuQuoin, IL | June 21-24 | 3551 | 102,543 | Rush Rush, Paula Abdul | Naked Gun 2 1/2 |
| 16th | 1992 | DuQuoin, IL | June 26-28 | 3583 | 106,025 | I'll Be There, Mariah Carey | Batman Returns |
| 17th | 1993 | DuQuoin, IL | June 25-27 | 3781 | 107,361 | That's the Way Love Goes, Janet Jackson | Poetic Justice |
| 18th | 1994 | DuQuoin, IL | June 24-26 | 3790 | 103,468 | I Swear, All-4-One | Lion King |
| 19th | 1995 | DuQuoin, IL | June 23-25 | 3712 | 106,953 | Have You Ever Really Loved a Woman, Bryan Adams | Apollo 13 |
| 20th | 1996 | DuQuoin, IL | June 21-23 | 3781 | 109,124 | Tha Crossroads, Bone Thugs-N-Harmony | Nutty Professor |
| 21st | 1997 | DuQuoin, IL | June 27-29 | 3709 | 105,623 | I'll Be Missing You, Puff Daddy & Faith Evans | Face/Off |
| 22nd | 1998 | DuQuoin, IL | June 12-14 | 3378 | 97,030 | The Boy is Mine, Brandy | Doctor Dolittle |
| 23rd | 1999 | Joliet, IL | June 25-27 | 2490 | 50,000 | If You Had My Love, Jennifer Lopez | Big Daddy |
|  | 2000 | NO EVENT | NO EVENT | 0 | 0 |  |  |
| 24th | 2001 | Indianapolis, IN | June 29-July 1 | 1682 | 32,300 | Lady Marmelade, Christina Aguilera, Lil' Kim, Mya & Pink | A.I. Artificial Intelligence |
| 25th | 2002 | Indianapolis, IN | June 28-30 | NP | NP | Foolish, Ashanti | Mr. Deeds |
| 26th | 2003 | Lima, OH | June 20-22 | NP | NP | 21 Questions, 50 Cent featuring Nate Dogg | Charlie's Angels: Full Throttle |
| 27th | 2004 | Lima, OH | June 18-20 | 791 | 14,738 | Burn, Usher | Farenheit 9/11 |
|  | 2005 | NO EVENT |  |  |  |  |  |
|  | 2006 | NO EVENT |  |  |  |  |  |
|  | 2007 | NO EVENT |  |  |  |  |  |
|  | 2008 | NO EVENT |  |  |  |  |  |
|  | 2009 | NO EVENT |  |  |  |  |  |
|  | 2010 | NO EVENT |  |  |  |  |  |
|  | 2011 | NO EVENT |  |  |  |  |  |
|  | 2012 | NO EVENT |  |  |  |  |  |
| 28th | 2013 | DuQuoin, IL | June 28-30 |  |  |  |  |

## Appendix C: Total Number of Pro Street Features By Year

|      | Car Craft | Hot Rod | PHR |
|------|-----------|---------|-----|
| 1977 | 6 | 4 | 4 |
| 1978 | 4 | 5 | 4 |
| 1979 | 6 | 7 | 4 |
| 1980 | 6 | 9 | 4 |
| 1981 | 12 | 10 | 7 |
| 1982 | 17 | 8 | 12 |
| 1983 | 17 | 33 | 30 |
| 1984 | 20 | 23 | 25 |
| 1985 | 51 | 40 | 24 |
| 1986 | 46 | 29 | 29 |
| 1987 | 37 | 43 | 33 |
| 1988 | 22 | 35 | 47 |
| 1989 | 31 | 48 | 60 |
| 1990 | 37 | 75 | 65 |
| 1991 | 32 | 97 | 54 |
| 1992 | 12 | 79 | 54 |
| 1993 | 12 | 63 | 26 |
| 1994 | 39 | 51 | 39 |
| 1995 | 14 | 16 | 31 |
| 1996 | 15 | 9 | 43 |
| 1997 | 8 | 13 | 25 |
| 1998 | 3 | 3 | 24 |

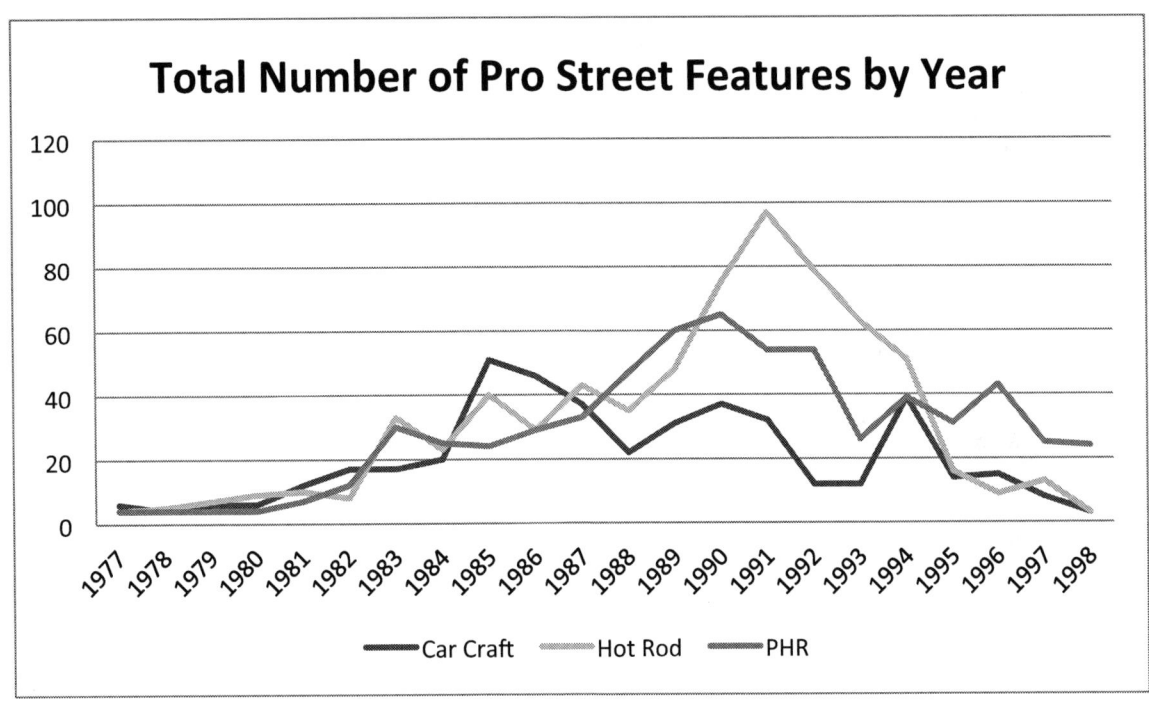

# Appendix D: % Total Features Pro Street By Year

|      | Car Craft | Hot Rod | PHR    |
|------|-----------|---------|--------|
| 1977 | 11.32%    | 3.57%   | 4.00%  |
| 1978 | 11.11%    | 3.11%   | 3.81%  |
| 1979 | 14.63%    | 4.17%   | 3.85%  |
| 1980 | 7.69%     | 6.57%   | 4.40%  |
| 1981 | 24.00%    | 8.62%   | 9.46%  |
| 1982 | 33.33%    | 7.69%   | 15.58% |
| 1983 | 25.37%    | 20.75%  | 37.04% |
| 1984 | 30.30%    | 19.17%  | 32.47% |
| 1985 | 52.04%    | 35.40%  | 30.77% |
| 1986 | 52.27%    | 26.85%  | 35.80% |
| 1987 | 51.39%    | 31.62%  | 31.73% |
| 1988 | 45.83%    | 33.98%  | 44.76% |
| 1989 | 62.00%    | 39.67%  | 60.61% |
| 1990 | 63.79%    | 53.96%  | 59.09% |
| 1991 | 56.14%    | 55.43%  | 50.00% |
| 1992 | 63.46%    | 45.93%  | 45.00% |
| 1993 | 37.50%    | 58.88%  | 23.85% |
| 1994 | 67.24%    | 51.00%  | 36.45% |
| 1995 | 35.00%    | 28.07%  | 34.83% |
| 1996 | 31.91%    | 23.08%  | 51.81% |
| 1997 | 24.24%    | 22.41%  | 41.67% |
| 1998 | 12%       | 6.25%   | 38.71% |